HANDBOOK OF MACAWS
H-1044

Photography

G.S. Axelrod: 7, 25 (bottom), 66, 74 (bottom left), 75, 83, 89, 90—birds trained by Shyne Browne, professional bird trainer for Sir Charles Pet Center; 24 (top), 25 (top), 64 (top), 74 (top left), 78 (bottom), 95 (top and center)—courtesy of Jeffrey and Mary Frohock at Aquarius, Ltd., 2190 East Atlantic Blvd., Pompano Beach, FL 33062; 33 (top). Dr. H.R. Axelrod: cover and endpapers, 11, 20 (top), 34, 35, 36 (bottom), 38, 43, 47, 49 (top), 52, 53 (top), 64 (bottom), 67, 71, 78 (top), 79, 95 (bottom), 106, 107, 115 (bottom). C. Bickford: 81 (top), 99. L. Brandt: 36 (top), 108. Dr. E. Burr: 42. R. Cathcart: 28, 29, 63, 69, 70, 84. A.R. Christian: 98 (top). R.A. Cook: 54, 55, 59. Dr. A.E. Decoteau: 114 (bottom). Courtesy of W.R. Grace and Co.: 53 (bottom). R. Hanson: 17, 20 (bottom), 21, 24 (bottom), 32, 115 (top), 119. A. Krausse: 13. H.V. Lacey: 46. P. Leyson: 56, 85, 91. J.D. Mikita: 12, 23 (bottom), 36 (center), 77. A.J. Mobbs: 10, 60 (top), 81 (bottom), 87 (top), 122 (top). Dr. J. Moore: 74 (right), 98 (bottom). Dr. E.J. Mulawka: 82, 102, 123. F. Nothaft: 16 (top). Courtesy of San Diego Zoo: 15, 39, 57, 93, 96, 103, 111. R. Small: 122 (bottom). Courtesy of Three Lions: 40, 44. L. Van der Meid: 19, 22, 26, 48, 49 (bottom), 50, 112. D. Vigliotti: 16 (bottom), 23 (top), 27, 31. Courtesy of Vogelpark Walsrode: 14, 30, 114 (top), 118.

Individuals shown in photos by G.S. Axelrod: Shyne Brown, 7, 25 (bottom), 89; Jeffrey Frohock: 24 (top), 25 (top); David Holzman: 7, 66, 75, 90; Pam Gamper: 64, 74, 78.

© 1982 by T.F.H. Publications, Inc. Ltd.

(t.f.h.)

ISBN 0-87666-844-9

Distributed in the U.S. by T.F.H. Publications, Inc., 211 West Sylvania Avenue, PO Box 427, Neptune, NJ 07753; in England by T.F.H. (Gt. Britain) Ltd., 13 Nutley Lane, Reigate, Surrey; in Canada to the pet trade by Rolf C. Hagen Ltd., 3225 Sartelon Street, Montreal 382, Quebec; in Canada to the book trade by H & L Pet Supplies, Inc., 27 Kingston Crescent, Kitchener, Ontario N28 2T6; in Southeast Asia by Y.W. Ong, 9 Lorong 36 Geylang, Singapore 14; in Australia and the South Pacific by Pet Imports Pty. Ltd., P.O. Box 149, Brookvale 2100, N.S.W. Australia; in South Africa by Valid Agencies, P.O. Box 51901, Randburg 2125 South Africa. Published by T.F.H. Publications, Inc., Ltd., the British Crown Colony of Hong Kong.

Handbook of Macaws

DR. A.E. DECOTEAU

Contents

Preface 9
KEEPING MACAWS
   The Macaws 11
   Feeding Macaws 16
   Housing Macaws 19
   Breeding Macaws 22
   Hand-feeding Baby Macaws 27
   Exhibiting Your Macaw 30
   Preventive Medicine 33
   Disease Conditions Affecting Macaws 41
SPECIES OF MACAWS
   Large Macaws 47
      Scarlet Macaw, *Ara macao*
      Blue and Gold Macaw, *Ara ararauna*
      Green-winged Macaw, *Ara chloroptera*
      Military Macaw, *Ara militaris*
      Hyacinth Macaw, *Anodorhynchus hyacinthinus*
      Red-fronted Macaw, *Ara rubrogenys*
      Caninde Macaw, *Ara caninde*
      Buffon's Macaw, *Ara ambigua*
      Lear's Macaw, *Anodorhynchus leari*
      Glaucous Macaw, *Anodorhynchus glaucus*
   Miniature Macaws 97
      Yellow-collared Macaw, *Ara auricollis*
      Severe Macaw, *Ara severa*
      Red-bellied Macaw, *Ara manilata*
      Noble Macaw, *Ara nobilis*
      Illiger's Macaw, *Ara maracana*
      Blue-headed Macaw, *Ara couloni*
      Spix's Macaw, *Cyanopsitta spixii*
   Hybrids and Extinct Macaws 121
Index 125

David Holzman and professional bird trainer Shyne Browne pose happily with two hyacinth macaws, two scarlet macaws and a blue and gold macaw in West Palm Beach, Florida.

Dedication

This book is dedicated to Kevin Paul Decoteau, my son, for his excellent support to me in the field of aviculture.

Acknowledgments

It is important that I thank Cliff Bickford for his continued support by offering some of the best photography seen in aviculture. It is also necessary to indicate how grateful I am to Rod Cathcart for the photos of trained macaws.

Preface

Over the centuries macaws have always been the parrots of choice for beauty and character. When the general public thinks of a parrot, they think of the beautiful scarlet and blue and gold beauties. Since these are long-lived birds, they were seen more often than other parrots in the 1940's and 1950's. This was due to the long ban by Public Health on parrot-type birds due to the fear of psittacosis, a respiratory disease of both birds and humans. With the advent of a simple antibiotic treatment for psittacosis, parrots (including macaws) were again allowed into the United States as pets.

By early 1970, macaws were being imported in great numbers. Prices remained low for only a brief period then, as time progressed, doubled and tripled. By the mid-seventies, the macaw population began to be controlled by certain exporting countries. The scarlet macaw became increasingly scarce, while its price continued to climb. On the other hand, by the fall of 1980, it was interesting to note that the price of blue and gold macaws fell. The popularity of the macaws remains steadfast since they are good pets, are easily trained, are extemely colorful and, in particular, are very loyal to their owners.

Blue and gold macaw, probably the most popular macaw.

Keeping Macaws

Military macaw, much in demand for a pet, though not brilliantly colored.

The Macaws

Perhaps the best known of all the parrots, the macaws have been pictured for centuries. They were paraded in a grand gesture by Columbus on his triumphant return from the New World and have been the pleasure of high courts of Europe.

The macaws are found from Mexico to Paraguay in South America and on Trinidad, an island just off the South American coast. Centuries ago macaws were found on other Caribbean islands, and there is evidence that a macaw was once a resident of St. Croix in the Virgin Islands.

My general classification of parrots lists ten major categories—true parrots, parakeets, lories, lorikeets, macaws, conures, cockatoos, cockatiels, lovebirds and parrotlets. Macaws are differentiated by the bare facial patch, the large bulky body and the very long elongated tail.

Of the 17 species of macaws in existence today, at least three and possibly five or six are considered extremely rare. The Spix's macaw, glaucous macaw, Lear's macaw, caninde macaw and the red-fronted macaw are included in this rare group.

Ten of the 17 macaws are classified as large, while seven are true miniature macaws.

Four of the listed macaws are entirely blue in color. The hyacinth, Lear's, glaucous and Spix's are blue and fit this category. All except the Spix's have a yellow facial patch; the Spix's has a black facial area. Seven of the macaws have rows of tiny feathers on the bare facial patch. These are the blue and gold, caninde, Buffon's, military, green-winged, red-fronted and severe. The severe is the only miniature having this characteristic. One miniature has a creamy yellow facial patch; this is the red-bellied macaw.

Macaws are thrilling to have around. It seems that the larger they are the easier they are to tame. Many of them learn to talk quite well. Their color is unequaled. Feathers from the macaws have been collected and treasured for centuries, and certain Indians still use them in glorious headdresses.

In comparison to some species of parrots, particularly the true parrots, the macaws are ready breeders in captivity. They lay eggs the size of bantam chicken eggs; as with all parrots, the eggs are white. In nature they are laid in a hollow tree or the equivalent, but aviculturists utilize wine barrels or garbage cans. Usually two or three eggs are laid.

Perhaps the most popular macaw in the late 1970's was the blue and gold, with over 3,500 of them imported into the United States in 1979. An indeterminate number were also hatched in captivity. The green-winged, military and scarlet are perhaps the next most popular, although the scarlet is getting increasingly rare.

Of all the parrots, the macaws are perhaps the most easily trained. Macaws are more frequently utilized in bird shows than are other parrots. Macaws have been trained to roller skate, ride bicycles, play cards, work puzzles and perform cute tricks appealing to the public.

The macaws are popular, as shown by recent increases in paintings, sculptures, models and novelties that have appeared in all types of stores for the public to purchase. Bath and beach towels, blankets and even sheets are decorated with colorful macaws. Friendly, loving, loud, mean, spiteful, colorful, appealing, docile and cautious are all characteristics often typical of the macaw.

Close-up of the head of a green-winged macaw.

Macaws are long-lived birds, if cared for properly. This is a blue and gold macaw.

The scarlet macaw, although still one of the most popular of the macaw species, is being kept less frequently by macaw fanciers.

Green-winged macaws are among the three macaw species that rank right behind the blue and gold macaw in popularity.

Feeding Macaws

Macaws must be fed somewhat differently than most other species of parrots because we (my family and I) believe that they have a greater need for protein than do most parrots. Although amazons also need higher protein, macaws have a greater need. For this reason we feed a variety of diets to our macaws, with stress on the amount of meat offered. Cooked (either fried or boiled) chicken is a favorite of macaws. They also love pork, particularly ham. Canned dog food that is high in both quantity and quality of meat is readily accepted. We feed a meat product as a delicacy two or three times a week. The total given in any one day is the equivalent of two tablespoons. If chicken (fried) is fed, we seldom give more than three ounces per feeding.

Our macaws are also extremely anxious to devour various fruits and vegetables, some of which they receive each day. We generally offer the equivalent of one pint of fruit or vegetables per day to each macaw. In pens or aviaries housing a pair of breeding macaws we double the amount to two pints.

We vary the fruit and vegetable diet by changing what is given each day. One day they get only apples; the next day they may receive our fruit combination, which is prepared in advance and frozen. We simply remove a package for complete thawing, then feed. Fruits in this combination package include apples, pears, grapes, oranges, lemons, grapefruits, cherries in season and papayas, as well as strawberries and blueberries in season. On another day we may feed corn on the cob (that has been frozen since the previous August) or canned corn. We allow the corn to thaw completely before feeding. Canned corn is easy to prepare—simply open the can and serve the corn and its juices in an open dish. On yet another day we may feed a stalk of celery to each macaw, with chicory or endive given the next time. Cooked sweet potatoes may be given at another time.

Food receptacles should be heavy enough or placed in such a way that they can not be easily tipped over.

Most macaws will eat out of their owner's hand—this hyacinth is no exception.

Using one foot to hold the food and the other foot to stand on a perch is no problem for a macaw. The T-stand is a particularly good place for a macaw because the bird has room to stretch its wings.

We have two basic diets that we feed on alternate days. Since we constantly improve our basic diets, the percentages of the ingredients change continually. At present one diet consists of 20% dog chow, 10% monkey chow, 30% safflower seeds, 30% sunflower seeds, with 10% red peppers and parakeet mix. (We also give monkey chow as choice tidbits each day, usually four to six chunks per bird.) The alternate diet is composed of 60% dog chow, 35% cooked rice, and 5% raisins, served by means of the rice water as a wet mash. New macaws must become accustomed to this mixture; they often refuse to eat it at first, but in due time they accept and relish it.

There are many ways to present grit or gravel to your macaws. Oyster shell is available, and various colors of grit can be obtained. We simply get a clean sandy soil out of our back yard. Grit helps make a stronger egg shell when your macaws lay. It is amazing just how much sand or grit is consumed.

We also feed vitamin and mineral supplements. Because there are numerous liquid and powdered vitamins and minerals on the market, you may need the help of a pet shop owner or your vet to decide which is the most suitable to use.

Constant review and improvement of diet is necessary. Too often today the cost of various food items has a bearing on feeding practices, leading to a reduced quality of diet.

Pet shops stock treats that may be fed to macaws. Various vitamin and mineral supplements are also available.

Housing Macaws

Housing is very important for both the pet macaw and the breeding macaw. If you have a pet macaw, it is important to look for a very large monkey cage or, better still, a specially made large macaw cage in which your macaw can spread its wings readily. Even more delightful for the pet macaw is the parrot stand. The macaw has the freedom of the stand and, unless it is an unscrupulous chewer, all will be well and the bird will be happy.

One of the many different styles of parrot stands. Most such stands are made of relatively hard woods to enable them to stand up to the gnawing to which they are subjected by macaws and other large parrots.

Constant study of our macaws has indicated that for the most part they exercise their wings frequently but move about the aviary very little. This is also true when you view macaws in a zoo. Many times I have seen macaws sitting in a barren, chewed-up tree with no interest in flying away. They prefer to screech at and preen each other.

In one of our aviaries, a pair of our scarlet macaws named John and Barney (John is the female) nested at ground level in a large hollow apple tree log. They spent all of their time at the log, with a few exceptions when they made trips (walking rather than flying) to the feeding and watering pans.

We prefer a black dirt base in most of our aviaries as the macaws get a lot out of digging in the dirt and fluffing their feathers like a chicken; in this way they secure a dry bath.

Our attempts at placing vegetation into macaw aviaries have been very unsuccessful, as the birds chew everything possible. We have to change wooden perches every two weeks or sooner, since they chew the perches into little pieces. We believe this is good for them so we do not complain. Because of macaws' chewing habits, though, one might be better off utilizing a chain link fence for the exterior of the macaw aviary. It is advisable to place branches in the aviary for their further chewing. We suggest that you do not use cherry wood—it could possibly be poisonous to your macaws.

This hybrid macaw is being trained by using the food reward system. Each time it performs the required behavior, it is given a bit of food.

This scarlet macaw is eating a grape. Macaws enjoy fruit and it is important to include it in their diet. The bird will remove the skin before eating the grape.

Macaws can use their feet almost as well as we can use our hands. Here a scarlet holds a peanut with its toes.

If you provide your macaws with a wooden nest box, the box should be reinforced with metal, as has been done with this nest box provided for a pair of ringnecked parakeets.

Breeding Macaws

Perhaps one of the easiest of the South American group of parrots to breed, macaws and their aviculturists have set records. The macaws are far easier to breed than are the amazons and are much easier to breed than are most conures. One must start with a true pair, male and female, of the proper age. In my opinion, macaws must be five to ten years of age before they will become effective breeders. They may well coax each other sooner and may even copulate, but in my experience eggs laid at a younger age are generally infertile.

One must ensure that adequate facilities are available for a pair of breeding macaws. We suggest they have ample room to spread their wings completely. A breeding pen seven feet high, five feet wide and eight feet long is very adequate. Since macaws are great chewers, do not use wood in the cage construction. We suggest using chain link or similar gauge fencing. Turkey fence, which is similar to hardware cloth, is also suitable because for some unexplainable reason they seldom bother it. If the macaws are content, they will remain inside without attempting to chew through the fencing, but they always chew wood. A large nest box must be placed in the aviary, preferably fairly high. If a wooden nest box is utilized, it will probably be chewed to pieces—unless it is reinforced with metal. Such a nest box should be a three-foot cube. We suggest taking a metal garbage can that is about four feet high, sealing on the lid, cutting a circular hole in the side and inserting a perch close to the hole. We place black greenhouse soil on the bottom of the nest can, with about two inches of pine shavings over the soil. The macaws will kick out the shavings they do not want.

We have utilized walk-in aviaries about 8 x 8 x 8 feet, with the height sometimes a bit more. We always give the birds two or three nests, either hollow logs or large garbage cans. The pair of macaws can then select their nest when they are ready. We place feeding stands just inside the door but use special openings since some breeding macaws can be very pugnacious.. The feeding and watering pans are placed at a medium height within the aviary.

We also use a reconstructed corn crib made out of steel. It is eight feet high but four feet square. Within this unit is a garbage-can nesting area. It has proved very suitable, having produced excellent nesting results with our blue and golds as well as our scarlet macaws.

At times an aviculturist can put together a male and a female of suitable age with neither one showing any apparent interest in the nest. It is a fact that occasionally a true pair will be incompatible. We have a quite old blue and gold female that recently received a new mate. She literally hates this male, and he doesn't care much for her either.

When a pair of macaws does finally become interested in the nest, you must prepare to feed more and better things. Protein is a necessity and must be increased.

When the eggs (generally two) are laid, you must make the decision whether to let the parents raise the young or to remove them for hand-feeding.

In summation, one can successfully breed macaws in fairly suitable units that are not enormous. Be sure they are not cramped and give them a lot of exercise, plenty of fresh water and lots of good food and attention.

Breeding a pair of macaws and successfully raising the young can be most gratifying. It is a challenge for anyone, whether he is a pet owner or an aviculturist of long standing.

A nine-and-a-half-week-old blue and gold macaw just feathering out.

Young macaws often have damaged tails when just out of the nest. These are young scarlets.

Tame macaws are great pets for young and old alike.

Once tamed, macaws will accept different types of handling from different people.

25

Sturdy aviaries such as this are suitable both for keeping and breeding macaws.

Hand-feeding Baby Macaws

Many times the aviculturist, the pet owner or the zoo wishes to remove newly hatched baby macaws from the nest in order to make them completely tame when fully grown. If indeed one does remove a baby or babies from the nest, then complete preparation must be made to ensure that the babies will do well. This takes a lot of time and much energy. At first one must be prepared to feed a warm food at least every two hours. You cannot get started and expect to spend six hours away at some party or function—unless you bring the babies along.

The most important part of the entire project is the feeding program one intends to utilize. Here are three feeding programs we utilize when we hand-feed. (However, we very seldom hand-feed because we are so extremely busy.)

In the first program we ensure that newly hatched babies receive only water for the first 72 hours. At about 72 hours of age we give them approximately two to three teaspoons of the following mixture, all blended into a pasty mush. *Formula No. 1:* 6 tbs. Cream of Wheat, 2 tbs. powdered milk, 3 tbs. ground sunflower hearts, 2 tsp. corn meal, 1 tbs. honey, 1 cup hot water.

The second formula we utilize is similar to the first; it has been one of the most effective diets. *Formula No. 2:* 6 tbs. Pablum, 2 tbs. powdered milk, 3 tbs. ground sunflower hearts, 1 tbs. honey, 1 jar mixed baby cereal with applesauce and bananas, 1 cup hot water.

The third diet is used on babies as they get older. *Formula No. 3:* 6 tbs. sunflower hearts, 6 tbs. safflower seeds, ½ cup powdered milk, 2 tbs. honey, 1 jar mixed baby cereal with applesauce and bananas.

One must be extremely careful to not overfill the crop of the baby with a hard mass. This could be the most dangerous problem encountered in hand-feeding. Where one does encounter crop binding, bring the heat up to about 90°F. and massage the crop gently. Give a few drops of a mixture of water and warm honey and gradually the solid mass will disappear. Hand-feeding baby macaws can be most rewarding, with the greatest reward coming when the babies are grown and completely hand-tamed.

The thrill of raising a baby macaw is evident here. This is a baby blue and gold.

28

Macaws can be trained to do many tricks. *Opposite:* A scarlet macaw riding a bicycle on a tight wire (above) and a scarlet showing that it knows where each card goes (below).
Right: A green-winged macaw, captain of his ship.
Below: A hybrid macaw on roller skates.

Exhibiting Your Macaw

Exhibiting your macaw can be much fun. You can attend many bird shows between September and December of each year, but you must start planning months in advance in order to show a macaw for the best results. Planning should begin by placing the macaw in the cage in which it will be shown. Various persons, preferably unknown to your macaw, should approach the cage so the macaw becomes used to strangers. Therefore, when the judge approaches the cage your macaw will show well without poor deportment. Deportment is indeed a feature the judge will look for at the exhibition. A macaw that retreats to the bottom of the cage or one that crawls all over the wires of the cage obviously lacks in deportment.

Conformation is also considered when macaws are judged. Does this particular macaw conform in symmetrical balance to the ideal? Is this macaw abnormally small for its standard size? Is the beak standard in growth and size with respect to the bird's body?

Condition is another important characteristic the judge must look for. Is the bird dirty about the tail or the body feathers? Are the wing or tail feathers damaged or fringed? Is the color of the bird vivid or dull?

Finally, how is the presentation of the bird? Is the macaw in a cage that is too cramped? Does he have room to turn around without damaging his long tail?

When you arrive at an exhibition, you must first complete an entry form and pay your entry fee. One then looks for the signs that indicate just where to bench the macaw. This is when an exhibitor can look at his competition. Most shows have a seating section where exhibitors and guests can watch the judging.

Bird shows are based on a procedure of gradual elimation. Macaws are first exhibited in competition against each other by breed, for instance scarlet macaw against scarlet macaw. Three placings are awarded; first takes a blue ribbon, second is red and third is generally yellow. The first-place macaw then competes against the Best Amazon, Best Conure, Best South American Parakeet and Best Caique for Best of the South American Parrots.

Exhibiting your macaw at a bird show can be an exciting and rewarding experience. Make sure that your bird is not flustered by strangers and that it is in top condition.

If by chance the Best Macaw succeeds as Best South American, then he competes for Best Parrot against Best South Pacific Parrot, Best Afro-Asian Parrot and Best Mutation Parrot. Best Parrot is then eligible to compete against Best Finch and Best Canary for Best in Show.

Different shows may have different rules, but most exhibitions result in a gradual elimination of all birds but one.

A head study of a magnificent blue and gold macaw.

Opposite:
Upper left: A close-up showing a peanut firmly grasped in a macaw's foot. *Upper right:* The macaw cracks the hard outer shell with its sharp beak and removes the kernel from inside with its tongue. *Lower left:* With its tongue, the macaw delicately removes the shell in one piece, discards the skin which it has removed completely and proceeds to eat the kernel. *Lower right:* A close-up of the peanut shows the results of this delicate operation and demonstrates the remarkable ability macaws have to use their feet in combination with their beak. Shown is the hard outer shell, cracked by the beak, the skin of the nut removed with the tongue, and the kernel, undamaged and ready to eat.

To maintain your macaw's good health, mineral supplements, in the form of mineral blocks (below) for example, should always be included in your bird's diet.

Preventive Medicine

Preventive medicine in macaws can be of utmost importance in maintaining good healthy birds that produce strong progeny. A source of potable water must be available 24 hours per day, and it must be changed every day. Trace minerals are important in the form of salt blocks for macaws. For years poultry fanciers have been feeding commercially mixed diets made up by trained nutritionists. Macaw breeders and owners are not so lucky, because usually they must mix their own diets. Too frequently these diets may lack the necessary vitamins and minerals, leading to a lack of protection against diseases or chemical and drug toxicity.

Vitamins are highly necessary in proper dosages, though too many vitamins may be as bad as an insufficient amount. Vitamin A serves to maintain the growth of cells covering body surfaces (called epithelial cells), while a deficiency permits them to be exposed to subsequent invasions of viruses and bacteria. Vitamin A can be derived from carotene, which is a pigment in some plants. Carotene is abundant in greens such as chicory and endive and in vegetables and fruits such as carrots and apples. Yellow corn is heavy with carotene, but other grains have little or none. Signs of vitamin A deficiency include watery diarrhea, discharge at the nares and dullness of feather colors. Lesions about the mouth and eyes will occur in acute cases.

Vitamin B requirements in macaws are small but essential. It is good to feed dog chow and monkey chow as well as dark bread to macaws; this will supply adequate amounts of the various B vitamins. In macaws, slowed growth of youngsters is the problem most frequently resulting from lack of vitamin B. Both parents must receive more of the above products to prevent this. Sunflower seeds are high in niacin, one of the B-vitamins.

Not all macaws are as colorful as this photo suggests. In comparison with hybrid macaws shown above, the red-bellied macaw shown on the opposite page is very plain.

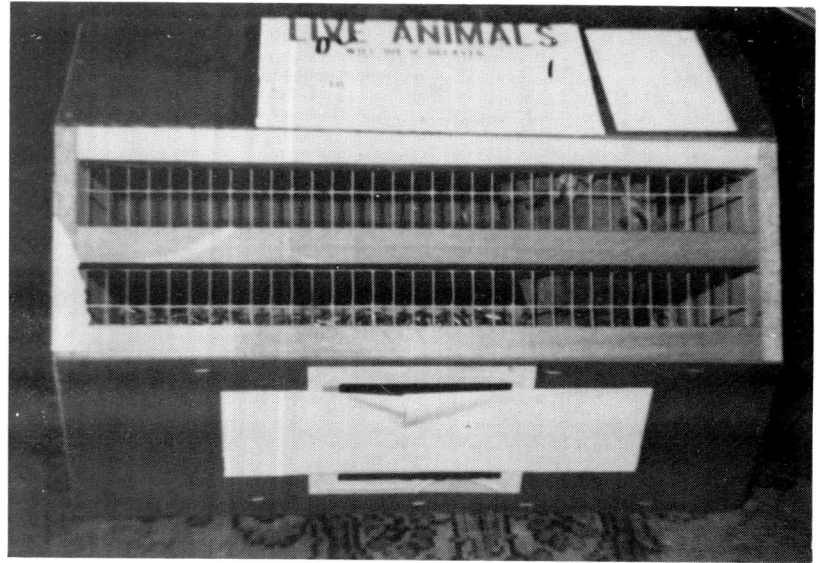

Most birds are shipped in a crate such as this. Upon arrival at its new home, the bird must immediately be removed from the crate.

Macaws should be housed in large cages and roomy aviaries to prevent tail damage evident on this scarlet macaw (right).

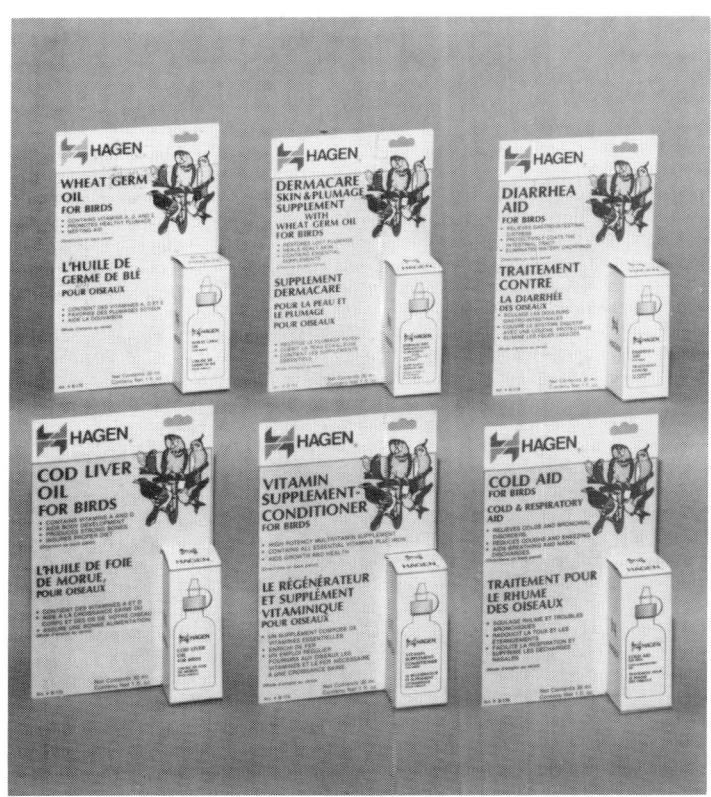

Your vet or pet shop owner will help you decide which of the many products made especially for birds would be best for your bird and its particular needs.

Vitamin D is readily synthesized by macaws that are maintained outside. Vitamin D is necessary for the proper absorption of calcium and phosphorus, elements needed for good bone development. Lack of vitamin D in indoor birds is readily noted in young birds when rickets develop. We suggest the addition of cod liver oil or turkey starter mash to the diet of indoor birds. These products contain sufficient vitamin D for most macaws.

When new birds are purchased, it is advisable to isolate them for 30 to 60 days well away from all other macaws. During this time, one must watch for nasal dripping, loose and watery diarrhea and other abnormal conditions. Always note the condition of the feathers. Continual fluffing of the feathers is always a bad sign. When fluffing of the feathers occurs, place the macaw in a very warm room, preferably 80 to 85°F. If nasal discharge or diarrhea should occur, immediately start the macaw on antibiotic therapy, preferably tetracycline in the drinking water. A sulphur-green diarrhea is often directly involved with a salmonella problem.

If you note anything too peculiar in the behavior or condition of your bird, you should secure assistance from a veterinarian noted for expertise in avian diseases. Good care, feeding the proper foods, early isolation of sick birds, and refraining from tramping through too many other aviaries constitute a good preventive disease program.

The blue and gold macaw (left and below) and the green-winged macaw (opposite) are among the species of macaws most frequently seen in captivity.

To restrict the mobility of un-caged birds, chaining is sometimes employed.

These green-winged macaws have had their ability to fly restricted by having one wing pinioned.

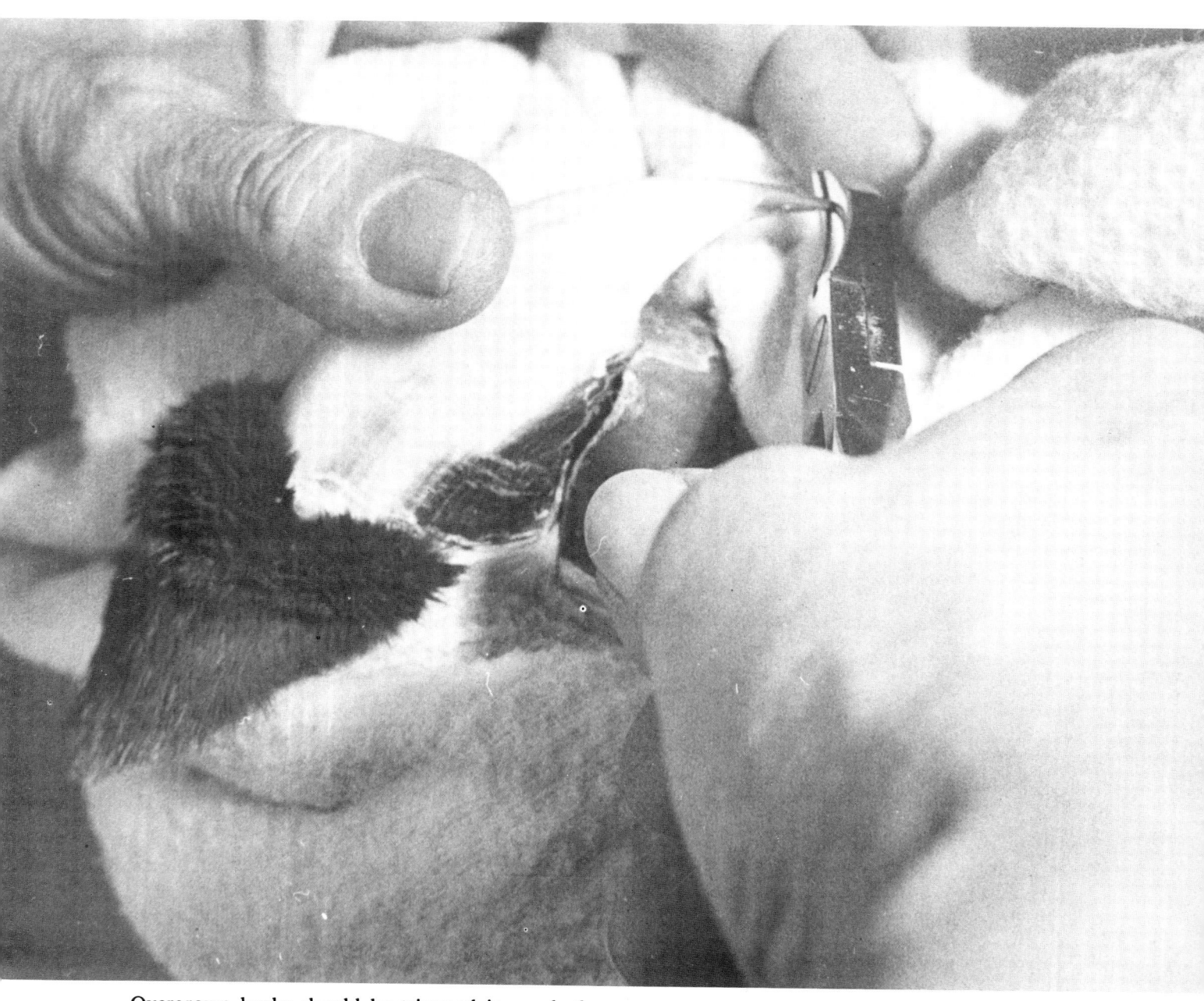
Overgrown beaks should be trimmed in much the same way as overgrown claws.

Disease Conditions Affecting Macaws

Fortunately, in my experiences with macaws I have encountered only very few problems involving diseases that affect these fabulous birds. I will attempt to cover only those conditions that have been of utmost importance in my aviaries.

By far the greatest problem encountered has been egg binding. Egg binding seems to occur with weather changes, but I have seen it in places that have been maintained at constant temperatures for some time. One can notice an immediate problem when the macaw fluffs up her feathers, appears listless and obviously strains. One must try to work closely with the macaw female in lubricating the vent with mineral oil, placing the bird in 90°F. surroundings and hoping for the appearance of the egg. If indeed she was already on one or two eggs (which happened to me one time), then these eggs should be removed for artificial incubation since the bird will seldom return to the nest. Enough stress has already occurred without the added stress of incubation. I once had an excellent breeder hen that became egg-bound after having laid two eggs. I was successful in retrieving the egg, but she never returned to the nest that particular session.

Feather plucking, or feather picking, is a problem with some macaws. It is not a problem involving nutrition. I believe it usually is a problem of either frustration or hormonal imbalance. There are anti-picking products sold in chicken or poultry supply houses that can be used on parrots. However, when one gives greater moving or flight room to a macaw and gives it something to chew on, most often the feather picking will disappear. One can give the macaw various toys to play with or chew up (such as large wooden blocks). At other times, nothing one can do will help. I know of one blue and gold macaw that lived for 25 years with her mate without ever plucking out one feather. After her

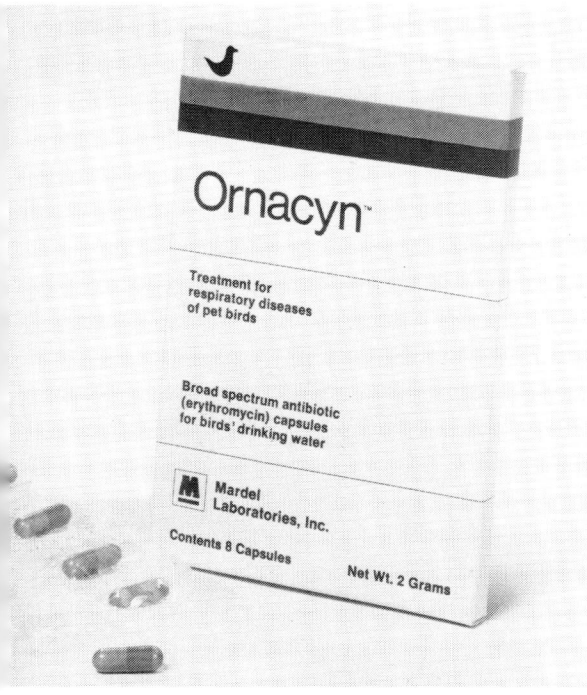

While certain antibiotics for birds are readily available at pet shops without prescription, they should be used only when necessary.

Mutual preening (above) is usual with macaw pairs. Lack of opportunity to engage in such behavior may be involved in some cases of self-plucking. The unsightly macaw shown opposite continually plucks the feathers from its breast.

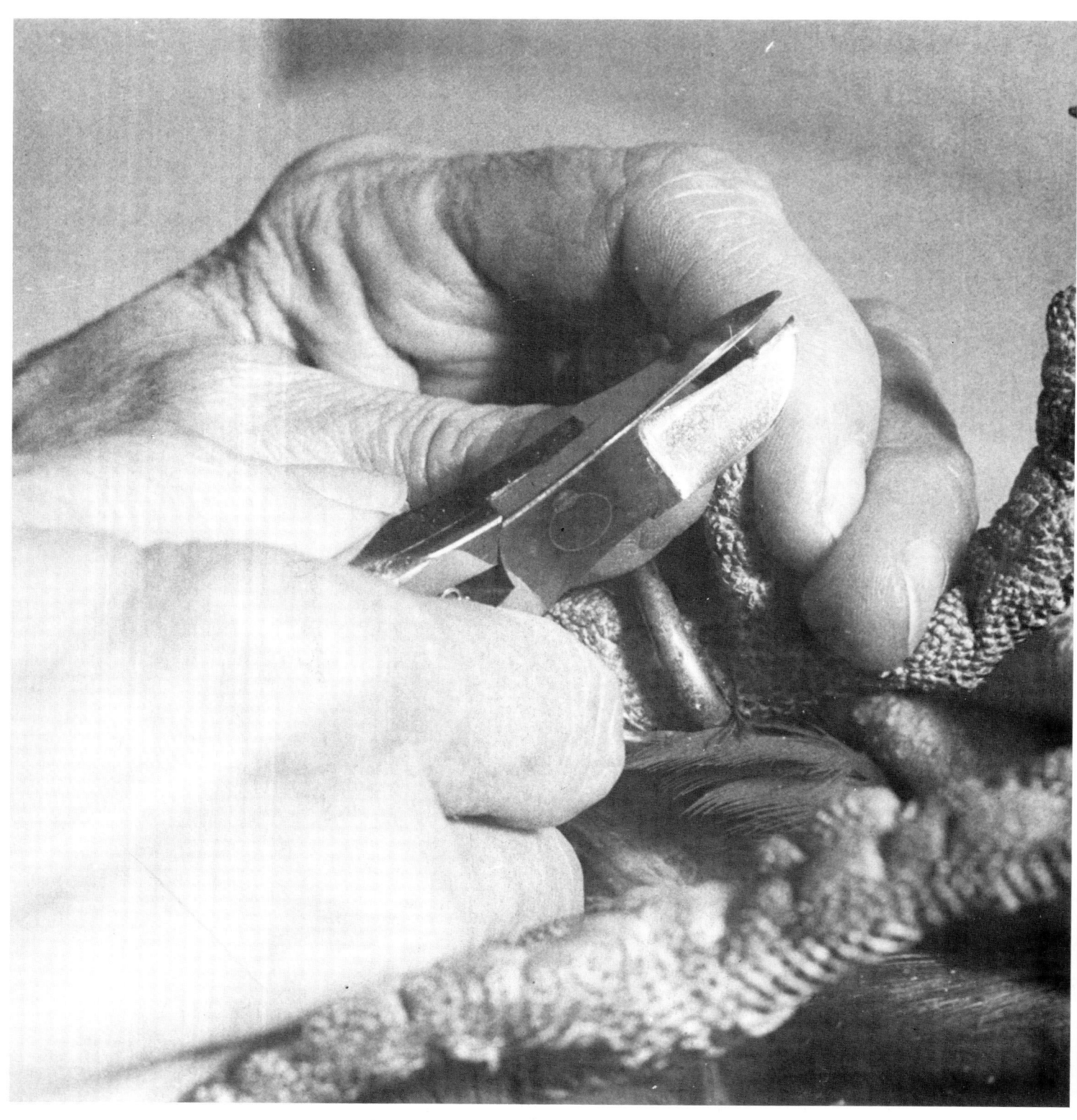

Claws must be trimmed very carefully. You don't want to cut the blood vessel which runs into each claw.

mate died, through her frustration she started plucking all the golden breast and abdomen feathers from her body. Giving her freedom of the entire yard had no effect on her feather plucking. To this day she remains a feather-plucker. Other instances of feather plucking have involved ectoparasites and impacted preening glands.

Long claws can be a problem on macaws. These can be trimmed, preferably with dog claw clippers. One must ensure that the claws are trimmed without cutting into the living tissue, otherwise the claw will bleed for a few minutes. If bleeding continues, simply dip the claw into some flour, which will aid clotting.

Other problems sometimes noted in macaws result from vitamin and mineral deficiencies that have gone too far. I have seen a few home-raised macaws with curly toes—this is a problem suggesting lack of B vitamins such as riboflavin and thiamine. Poor feathering or stunted feathers may be due to lack of B vitamins including riboflavin, but could also be due to a lack of protein. In some newly imported macaws we have seen abnormally scaly legs and scabs on the head, eyes and about the corners of the beak. This is related to lack of vitamin A and various B vitamins such as biotin and riboflavin as well as pantothenic acid.

One must always select a veterinarian with much expertise in avian medicine who can see your bird at short notice—birds can die very quickly. Time is always precious when something is wrong, and quick action has saved good birds in the past and will continue to in the future.

If bleeding does occur while you are clipping a claw, use flour or a styptic powder to stop the flow of blood.

Species of Macaws

The following sections treat each species of living macaw. The species are grouped first by size—large versus miniature—and then by general popularity in each size group.

Large macaws convey through their posture while resting the impression that they are calm and unafraid, as the scarlet macaws shown below and opposite demonstrate.

Large Macaws

Scarlet Macaw, *Ara macao*

Perhaps the most famous of all the macaws, the scarlet has been known for centuries and is probably better known to the general public than almost any other species of the parrot family.

The scarlet macaw has a large geographical home, having been found from Mexico to southern Brazil as well as on Trinidad. It is thought that the scarlet macaw was found on many Caribbean islands up to two centuries ago, but it is now extinct there, if it ever really did occur. They are dwindling in numbers in many parts of the great South American frontiers, and it is difficult to find the scarlet in Mexico anymore.

Too frequently the general public believes the diminishing population of scarlet macaws and other parrots in the natural areas of origin is due to the taking of young babies from the nesting holes. The fact is that the clearing of land for the further planting of bananas, coffee, etc., does much more damage to the scarlet macaw's habitat. Aviculturists must be allowed to breed scarlet macaws for the future of the macaw and mankind. The scarlet macaw is a good breeder in captivity.

The scarlet macaw is a colorful bird. There are no rows of small feathers on the bare facial patch. The orange red or scarlet color covers the entire body except for the bright blue rump. Both wings are bright yellow, with the lower secondary and primary feathers dark blue.

Supply and demand always control the price of everything, including the scarlet macaw. In 1974, one could purchase a scarlet for $500.00 to $600.00 each; by 1978 they were $800.00 to $900.00. In 1979 it was difficult to find a scarlet at $1,000.00, and by the end of 1980 the price varied from $1,500.00 to $1,800.00 each. Tame and talking scarlets were much higher priced.

As a pet, the scarlet macaw is most exciting. They can be taught to talk very well and can be tamed to be easily handled. We have one called Barney who loves to roll over and over then get up and say, "Hello, baby." They love to show off. Once you begin training them, they will not forget. Scarlet macaws have been trained to roller skate, to ride a small bicycle, to walk a tightrope and to select colored pieces of various shapes for the proper holding receptacle.

Opposite: This hybrid macaw has been trained to fly to its owner's arm whenever its name is called.

This scarlet macaw is engaged in preening its tail coverts.

There are two major methods of training. One involves giving the bird a treat as a reward when it performs well. Many trainers withhold sunflower seeds from macaws they train until it is needed for a reward. They love sunflower seeds so very much that they certainly will learn quickly for a taste of that sunflower seed.

The other method is the kindness system. When the scarlet macaw does a creditable job on any training stint, the scratching of its head is often worthwhile. This they thoroughly enjoy.

My son Daren has been training macaws for some time utilizing both methods. His work with a scarlet macaw called John has been most effective. John loves to roll over and play dead. Then when picked up, she (yes, John is female) enjoys being swung around and

While tending the aviary of a pair of breeding scarlet macaws, careful watch is kept on the birds. Macaws resent intrusion and are liable to attack anyone entering their aviary during the breeding season.

around by her legs. She then snuggles up to the chest of her trainer and says, "Hello, I'm here." John is also an exceptional showbird and always seems to be in excellent feather. In 1978, John was Second Best in Show at two successive shows with 740 and 480 birds entered. John had been Second Best in Show at least once before, but she has never yet won Best in Show. Her color, conformation and condition are always very good, which is why she has done so well. One judge badly wanted to purchase John, but needless to say the bird is not for sale.

It is unfortunate that scarlet macaws are not exhibited in greater numbers at the shows. One reason, of course, is the necessity for a large show cage—some magnificent cages have been utilized for exhibit, as well as large dog cages. Even at the national bird show there were not over two or three scarlet macaws present. In 1980, there were no large macaws present in the three large northeastern shows in October.

As a breeder the scarlet macaw is prolific, so many scarlet macaws have been bred in the United States. We have been successful on numerous occasions with our two pairs of scarlets. Generally, scarlet macaws will lay either two or three eggs to a clutch, and in our case one pair consistently produces three white eggs, while the other pair lays two.

It is seldom that these eggs do not hatch. The tiny, naked, sightless babies are as ugly as one can imagine. Our parents are excellent in feeding their young, par-

A pair of scarlets. The bird on the left is thirty years old and is a feather plucker in the spring. The rest of the year she is fully feathered.

ticularly since we feed the adults much meat and cheese in addition to the regular diets listed elsewhere in this book. The babies are extremely slow in emerging as fledglings from the nest; it takes almost 90 days before our babies emerge. When they do emerge, they are so heavy that they are often larger than the parents, but in due time they lose this baby fat.

Macaws that are breeding can be extremely pugnacious and will attack after fair warning if one approaches the nest. I well remember some years ago a pair of scarlets at the Cleveland Zoo that had a nest on the ground. There was a lean-to in a gravel area under which the scarlets had two eggs. Upon our approaching it, the male waddled over to us with hackles up, screeching a warning to stay away. The tamer the macaw, the more dangerous it is when breeding or nesting.

Several friends have had success breeding scarlet macaws. One such friend, Harold Bradley from Ohio, was most successful with his pair of scarlet macaws. They were babies when he purchased them in 1964, but it wasn't until 1974 that they showed any interest in breeding, although a large nest box had been available to them for years. When they finally did get serious, they laid only one egg. This egg was guarded with much jealousy for weeks but never hatched. They tried again in six or seven months and the same thing happened: one egg that didn't hatch. The egg was fertile each time, but it appeared that the chick died halfway through incubation. Harold was beyond reproach. He tried changing diets, he sprayed the adults with warm water twice per day, and he added vitamins to the diet. When he finally increased protein intake (after two more unsuccessful nests), the macaws finally laid two eggs, both of which hatched. Harold has had good luck ever since.

Another friend in Puerto Rico allowed his macaws (two scarlets) to roam his premises at will. He had no notion of their age because they had been purchased from a local zoo east of San Juan. This pair nested in a garbage can in a back room. They laid three eggs, all of which hatched. The owner hand-fed the babies and made superb pets of them. Interestingly, the adult pair fed entirely off the land from the many fruit trees on the property. They also had available several types of roots similar to potatoes and yams.

Other friends in Florida have six pairs of scarlet macaws that produce readily and frequently. They hand-feed all their babies. It is a thrill to see boxes of baby macaws of all sizes and ages literally all over the house!

The temperament of scarlet macaws allows them to be kept uncaged. Most of the time they are content to climb about or remain on perches.

Blue and Gold Macaw, *Ara ararauna*

There are many people that faithfully believe the blue and gold macaw is the best and favorite of all macaws. Certainly the contrast of the blue and the golden yellow is most fascinating.

Blue and gold macaws are indeed attractive, with the front of the head greenish blue turning bright blue on the crown and back. The chin under the beak is black, with a brilliant yellow breast and abdomen. Truly a blue and *gold!*

In contrast to the scarlet macaw, the wholesale price of the blue and gold macaw has been dropping. In 1974, blue and golds were selling for $800.00 to $1,000.00. By 1978 they were $700.00 to $900.00, and by the fall of 1980 one could purchase at wholesale a blue and gold for $350.00 to $500.00. By the end of the 1970's, blue and gold macaws were imported in greater quantities than any of the other larger macaws.

As a pet, the blue and gold macaw is excellent. One is better off purchasing a baby blue and gold macaw that has been hand-fed by the breeder. These are easier to train and easier to teach how to talk.

One lady in New England owns a magnificent blue and gold by the name of Woody. This bird is extremely tame and insists on riding on one's shoulder constantly. He is unique in being an escape artist and has even opened a padlock. His favorite food is a bunch of grapes. After going through a lock for the grapes, he will devour them in haste. This bird loves people; surprisingly there are many blue and golds that fit this category.

Perhaps one of the most favored blue and golds that I know is owned by my son Daren. This is a magnificent charmer called Charlie. Charlie came to us several years ago with a superior history. The bird was brought into a southern bird farm 47 years ago and remained at the premises for 27 years. During this period Charlie selected a mate, another blue and gold. Through the years this pair raised several babies. Charlie, a female, always laid two eggs to every clutch. Then, during the 25th year, Charlie's mate suddenly died. Within the next few months Charlie started feather-plucking her breast feathers. The depressed owners sold Charlie, as she was soon completely bare-breasted, pulling each new pin feather that appeared. Charlie was purchased as part of a lot of birds by a zoo somewhat farther north, and for ten years she was kept behind the scenes in a cage by herself. She despised the zoo director but loved two of the keepers.

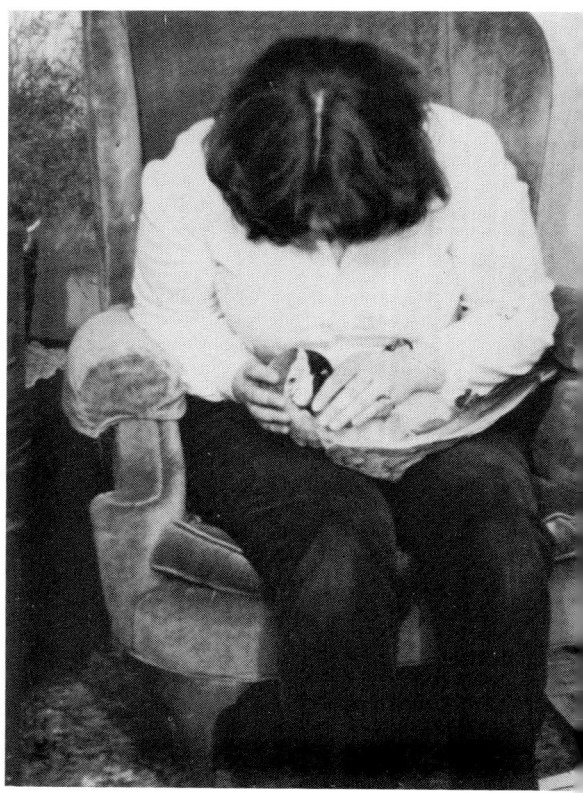

Lying in its owner's lap is a favorite activity for this blue and gold macaw.

This tame blue and gold waits patiently while its owner fixes a perch in its cage.

This macaw is very tame and trusts its owner to handle it with care.

A display of shared affection.

Above and opposite: Blue and gold macaws.

On one of our visits to the zoo, we noticed the forlorn blue and gold with no golden feathers in view. Apparently, through the years knowledge of Charlie's sex had been lost and no one was sure whether she was a male or a female, though they thought Charlie was a male. We decided we could have fun with Charlie, so we made a decent trade. To date Charlie remains a feather-picker, but one wonders why. She has the run of the entire yard, all four acres. She flies around the entire house, lands on the roof and thoroughly enjoys herself. She loves our sons, particularly Daren, and protects him frequently.

Charlie loves to go for open-toed shoes, then bites the wearer's big toe. More friends and relatives have been bitten by Charlie than I care to remember. Charlie does not particularly like strangers but will sit on the arm of certain friends of Daren. Daren, of course, can ride his bicycle with Charlie on the handlebars enjoying every bit of it. Daren can literally do anything he wishes to with Charlie. He carries Charlie under his shirt, occasionally with a blue head peering out. Frequently, when relaxing in the yard Charlie will join us by climbing up on our lawn chairs, enjoying a perch beside one of the family. On the arrival of one of the neighbors or another stranger, though, Charlie's hackle feathers go up straight. This is her fair warning.

One October day, I returned from a trip to San Diego to find that Charlie had laid two (infertile) eggs that she jealously guarded much too long. We decided it was time Charlie had a new mate, but Charlie loved people too much and never accepted the male. They constantly fight. Could it be that Charlie is just too spoiled?

As breeders they are very active birds. There have been many blue and gold macaws bred in captivity. Ed Diffendale has been most successful in breeding the blue and gold utilizing a garbage can as a nesting unit. Both parents spent much time within the nest, where they frequently laid clutches of three eggs. Ed fed chicken meat quite often, which appeared to help the parents very much.

Our successes with blue and golds were generally good. Our breeding pair enjoyed cheese and both dry and canned meaty dog food. They both fed their babies efficiently, spending much time in their garbage can nest. Both of the parents are extremely pugnacious to all persons, including the hands that feed them. Their eggs and their babies are under their guard, and let no one interfere.

Jerry Pitton of Arizona has a unique situation with six mated pairs of blue and gold macaws, each pair in a

9 x 9 x 9-foot chain-link pen. The pens are side by side. Two nesting logs are located in each pen. The most interesting aspect of their behavior involves the mannerisms of each pair. When one pair starts the royal courtship, within days so do all the others. Within a matter of two weeks all six pairs of blue and golds are nesting on two or three eggs each. This has happened on at least three occasions.

A blue and gold enjoying flying with the help of its owner.

Jerry's feeding practices were somewhat different but interesting. His basic diet consisted of safflower and sunflower seeds at a 50:50 ratio. He feeds much fruit and many vegetables. The fruit is diced into chunks and consists of papaya, melon, grapes, bananas, oranges, lemons and grapefruit. He cooks all of his vegetables, mostly by baking. The main selections include sweet potatoes, white potatoes, turnips, carrots and a large white root I have not heard of before that looks like a giant potato and has white flesh. Apparently his macaws do well on this diet as he has much success in raising the young, all of which are fed and raised by the parents.

The blue and gold macaw in the show ring is a fine exhibition bird if properly shown in good feather and condition and also in the appropriate caging. Like the scarlet, few blue and golds are seen at the bird shows, with seldom more than two or three at most shows. Perhaps as shows become increasingly popular we will see more large macaws on display.

The black facial feathers of the blue and gold macaw, one of its most striking characteristics, are already evident on these five-week-old nestlings.

As blue and gold macaws grow older, the black facial feathers become more sharply defined, as evidenced in the birds shown at left and opposite.

Green-winged Macaw, *Ara chloroptera*

Although the green-winged macaw should be the aristocrat of the macaws, it has just never quite succeeded. To me this is a majestic, large, beautiful bird. In contrast to the scarlet, which is often confused with the green-winged by the general public, this macaw has a much larger head, is an overall larger bird and has a facial patch with rows of tiny red feathers. The red of the green-winged is crimson, a beautiful darker red, and, of course, there is no yellow on the wings, simply blue and green. This magnificent bird unfortunately takes a back seat to the scarlet and the blue and gold macaws in popularity.

There are some breeders and aviculturists, however, who have been very successful with the green-winged macaw. It makes a fine pet and, if trained early, makes an excellent hand-tame one. I have seen pet green-winged macaws that were easily handled and had a pretty good vocabulary.

One young man in Rhode Island started with a fully grown macaw that he had purchased from a pet store. This bird could not be handled and was frightened of people. The young owner started with heavy gloves and a perch-like stick. Within a few days the bird, named Tommy, began to step onto the stick. Within another week the man could take Tommy out of his cage on the stick. By friendly coaxing he was soon able to scratch the bird on the head. Then he attempted to use his gloved hand in place of the stick with good luck. After numerous attempts, this young owner was able to take off the gloves when placing his arm into the large cage; immediately Tommy would put his large beak down for leverage (one would think at first that he was about to bite). Patience and no quick movements were fruitful, and Tommy proceeded to perch on his owner's arm. This was a major breakthrough and a beginning to a long, pleasant training program. In due time Tommy was completely hand-trained and began to talk as well as perform a few tricks. This success story is proof that patience can produce results.

I periodically hear stories about parrots and cats. John Netliomi of New Jersey has about the best one I have heard. He not only has a green-winged macaw but a white Persian cat as well. Both the bird and the cat have the run of the house. The cat loves to paw at the tail of the macaw, and the macaw, in turn, loves to go for the tail of the cat. It is most fascinating and comical to see this circle of excitement that lasts until the cat screams due to a severe and hard bite on the tail. Occasionally a tail feather is lost, but the macaw always fares better in the outcome. One time the cat was too forward; the macaw bit down too hard, and off came the end of the tail. This incident did not deter the cat from future attempts, though, and over a period of years with back and forth teasing the owner ended up with a bobtail Persian cat and a tailless green-winged macaw. The only difference is that the macaw's tail always grows back.

The green-winged macaw has been successfully bred on many occasions in the United States. Almost universally, however, owners have told me that the general age of the breeding pairs was never less than six or seven years. This again bears out my opinion that macaws must be five or six years old or perhaps even older to be successful as breeders.

With a little help, this green-winged macaw successfully plants a flower.

Harry Ramber of Michigan has one pair of green-winged macaws that were 12 and 15 years of age when they finally went to nest in a garbage can; the female was the older of the two. They were together for seven years before taking any interest whatsoever in the nesting area. The owner had started with a large hollow log, but never one spark of interest was shown by the birds. I suggested that he take a large garbage can, seal the cover on and make a large hole in the side for a decent entrance, ensuring that a perch be placed just below the hole entrance. They still didn't do anything for a couple of years; apparently they were just not ready.

Harry's feeding methods differ considerably from ours. He uses much in the lines of greens and vegetables,

Note the distinctive yellow on the wing and the orange-red color of the head, back and tail of this scarlet macaw.

Scarlet is also the predominant color of the undersides of the wing and tail of both the scarlet and the green-winged macaws.

with chicory, endive and cabbage given daily. I had not witnessed cabbage being used frequently before, but surprisingly his macaws enjoy cabbage very much. He feeds much cucumber and corn, as well as shredded carrot by the bushel. Harry's vocation is related to raising vegetables; his seconds go to the birds. It interested me that they enjoyed cucumbers that were juicy and evidently tasty. We only give the large, yellow, over-ripe cucumbers at our aviary, the ones we do not use for human consumption. (Generally our fruits and vegetables are always the finest, selected for our own consumption.) In addition to vegetables, Harry feeds sunflower seeds and dry dog food.

He has had great success. His pair, when finally into production, laid two eggs on the first nesting. Unfortunately neither egg hatched. Nine months later, they made another attempt with two more eggs; this time both hatched. Since Harry removes his babies from the nest and hand-feeds his babies, he is totally successful.

Green-wings are indeed as lovable and enjoyable as any other type of macaw. They seem to enjoy producing the eggs, hatching them and feeding and raising babies for your enjoyment. Renee LeRoy had two most attractive green-winged macaws for several years. They appeared as loving to each other as any pair could possibly be. They copulated frequently, yet they never entered the nesting hole. With the advent of the endoscope, Renee decided to have her two green-wings sexed. Her veterinarian advised her that she owned two males!

This is an age-old story that I have seen happen time and time again. Two females will also copulate, and they may also "play" at nesting. I guess that unless you have a pair that produces actual babies or fertile eggs, you can never be sure of the sex of the pairs. Keep in mind that in the world of birds it is often said that "A pair consists of two birds."

Mike Mavilia of Massachusetts had one of the most attractive green-winged macaws I have ever seen. This was a beautiful, large, massive, well-feathered macaw that was tame and easily handled. He was well kept by Mike in a huge pen. It is a pleasure to see such a nice bird.

Mary Mapleton has two pairs of green-winged macaws. She had made a thrilling trade to a zoo for the four birds, trading two of her young wallabies for the macaws. Evidently the zoo had maintained these macaws for many years with no apparent attempt at breeding them. Mary has had excellent success in raising babies from these two pairs, especially as she surprisingly received two true pairs! All it took was a few nesting boxes for them to become active.

A blue and gold and two scarlet macaws enjoying the company of their owner.

Although green-winged macaws make excellent pets and are beautiful birds, they have never been as popular as scarlets and blue and golds.

Military Macaw, *Ara militaris*

Not as popular and not as colorful as the scarlet, green-winged and blue and gold, the military macaw is still a beautiful bird. The brilliant red forehead is a typical color trait of the military. The dark green body color is a strong differentiating characteristic from the yellowish green of Buffon's macaw, which is so nearly a twin of the military. The wings have a beautiful aqua color, the tail coverts are light blue, and red suffuses most of the tail feathers. The exquisite rows of tiny black feathers over the bare white facial patch is another typical trait of the military macaw, as well as the Buffon's.

This is another one of the large macaws so much in demand. As a pet the military is quite desirable. Apparently the military is still fairly plentiful in parts of Mexico. When I was in Tijuana in early 1979 I purposely visited the farmers' markets on the off streets where there are not quite as many tourists. The varied parrots and softbilled birds for sale were plentiful, however, and once you showed an interest in purchasing birds they seemed to come out of the woodwork.

One Mexican had a quite nice military macaw. It was in a large cage in the corner of a store very full of merchandise, along with several large, black cages. He was asking $75.00 for the bird. Another businessman took us through a back yard to a long passageway, through a locked gate, and then to a private home where there were four semi-tame military macaws. He was willing to sell them for $60.00 each. Since I had to leave San Diego by air for home and had no plans to return to pick up quarantined birds, I was not interested. However, the two parties with me purchased two macaws with the understanding they would pick them up the next day so they could take them to the San Ysidro quarantine station for their thirty-day stay. When they returned to secure a health certificate from the Mexican veterinarian, they were told they needed a Mexico City permit to export them. They were also told it might take six months or a year before they received a permit. Consequently, they had to resell the birds for a loss and ended up taking only a large cage (at a loss) home with them.

There are pet owners who have one military macaw and no others. Their selection of foods includes sunflower seeds, peanuts as treats, carrots, apples and greens such as endive and chicory; they also feed celery. Their military macaw apparently fares quite well on this diet, but aviculturists who readily breed birds would not consider this a complete diet for their breeders. As a pet diet, though, we think it is satisfactory.

Military macaws have been known to be excellent pets, are easily handled and have the ability to perform various tricks. I know of one military macaw that can roller skate, as well as play cards, select puzzles, differentiate colors and dance, and roll over. There is another military macaw, owned by a very elderly couple in their late eighties, that can pick almost any padlock around. This is one of his favorite pastimes and gives his owners hours of relaxation. His name is "Picka," which is quite appropriate.

Barry Renton of New Hampshire has a military macaw, one of four parrot pets, that eats only people food. He loves mashed potatoes, devours roast beef and fried chicken and enjoys feeding on peas, carrots and turnips that have been cooked. His favorite, however, is glorified rice, a concoction of rice, pineapple and whipped cream. This will keep him happy for hours.

The military macaw has been bred in the United States on several occasions. Those aviculturists that I am acquainted with tell me that the military is not quite as pugnacious when breeding as is the scarlet, the blue and gold and the green-winged. Whether this is universally true only future experiences will tell us.

Bea Bentran, an avid aviculturist from California, has informed me that her pair of military macaws is having annual successes in a wooden beer barrel. Two items surprised me: one was the use of a wooden barrel without extensive chewing by the macaws, and the other involved the calmness of her macaws. They laid two eggs each clutch, with both chicks hatching every time. She left the chicks to the parents for feeding. Both parents spent much time in the nest feeding the two babies; the increase in sunflower seeds devoured was

It's puzzle time for this military macaw.

Green-winged macaw teasing a pretty lady.

This green-winged has the right idea about planting a flower, but he has the wrong end up.

The same macaw getting more water for the flower.

The military macaw is smaller than Buffon's macaw, a bird with which it is often confused. The green on the back and neck of a Buffon's also has more yellow in it than that on a military. Shown here is a military macaw.

three-fold. She also fed many apples and pears and, when available, much celery as well as cottage cheese. She claims the cottage cheese makes a great deal of difference in the rapid growth and feathering of her macaw chicks. Before she started feeding large helpings of cottage cheese, her babies fledged at 80 to 90 days. Now that cottage cheese is added as a feeding supplement for the parents, she has been surprised to see the fledged babies appear from the nest at 75 to 80 days.

There are three subspecies of the military macaw. The already described nominate subspecies, *Ara militaris militaris*, is found in Colombia and adjacent Venezuela, Ecuador and Peru. This subspecies is somewhat smaller than the other two, although not by much. It is very difficult to differentiate this subspecies from the larger subspecies from Mexico, *Ara militaris mexicana*. The latter bird is found in the oak and pine forests from Sonora to Oaxaca, Mexico. The third subspecies, *Ara militaris boliviana*, is found in Bolivia and adjacent Argentina and is distinguished from the other two subspecies by a reddish brown throat coloring. Only about 5% of the military macaws imported into the United States are of the subspecies *boliviana*. It is interesting to note this difference, as I have seen an occasional pair that consisted of two different subspecies. The reddish brown throat of *Ara militaris boliviana* is unique and easily noted.

One such mixed pair is owned by Paul Palley in Illinois. I was quite eager for his pair to breed and produce young to see what coloring they might have. Paul did have success after four years of trying. He was told the birds were ten or more years of age when he purchased them, so if that was correct, this pair did not breed until they were well over 14 years of age. Paul had been told they did not breed for the previous owner.

Eventually the pair produced two eggs. It seemed to Paul that it was an endless wait between the time the eggs were laid and the hatching, and it was even longer between the time of hatching (both eggs hatched) and fledging. However, one fine morning Paul called me to report that the two babies had finally appeared out of the nest box. They both had dark reddish brown throats, which may be indicative that the trait is dominant. It would be interesting to secure more information from various pet owners, breeders and aviculturists on breeding pairs and their progeny to see just how many Bolivian birds are in the hobby.

Hyacinth Macaw, *Anodorhynchus hyacinthinus*

The largest of the macaws as well as the largest of the parrots is the majestic and most unique hyacinth macaw. This bird is large and awe inspiring but also very docile when handled appropriately. The beautiful dark blue hyacinth color over the entire body is in contrast to the bare yellow facial patch. The size of the patch can be enlarged or decreased by movements of the mandibles.

The hyacinth is found mainly in a large area of Brazil southeast of the Amazon. It is thought by many that there are no self-sustaining flocks in other countries of South America, but we believe there are two, one in Paraguay and one in Colombia. I have this from two South American ornithologists who are highly thought of in bird circles. Whether the birds are native to these countries or were introduced is unknown.

As pets they are beyond reproach. I have found some of the best-behaved, tamest, well-trained macaws to be hyacinths. One friend in New Hampshire has a very steady, colorful and friendly hyacinth. This young bird, hatched in the U.S., is very easily handled. She loves to kiss her owner, then walk on his arm, jump to the other arm and climb to his shoulder. This bird is unique in that it has a fifth toe on one foot. What a unique identification method! As you know, all parrots have two toes pointing forward and two toes pointing backward. This extra toe is to the rear.

Another friend, also in New Hampshire, has a magnificent, large hyacinth macaw, a male. This bird was sexed by the endoscopic method. Although Bill, the owner, does not have another parrot, he still had the bird sexed. In all fairness, this hyacinth is an extremely talented pet. He has been taught to climb a ladder to the top, go down the other side and then return up and down again. The bird also plays ball with the family dog and the family. He loves to play cards, seemingly knowing which is the ace in each category. He can also be a pest, as he loves to turn the television on and off and even has the ability to switch the channels. This hyacinth macaw has a taste for the unusual and is completely spoiled by his owner. His favorites are ice cream bars and wieners. He averages a wiener a day and makes a royal mess with the ice cream bar.

We once visited a facility for holding parrots prior to sale to pet shops, breeding farms, and brokers. One large pen held at least twenty magnificent hyacinths. Their menu was interesting to note. Fresh coconut cut

Left and below: By moving its mandibles, the magnificent hyacinth macaw can change the shape and size of its yellow facial patch.

This hyacinth macaw exhibits the calm and poise typical of a trained macaw.

The pleasure that tame macaws can provide is evident in this gentleman.

up in chunks in the shell was the main diet, with Brazil nuts given every afternoon at the rate of six per hyacinth. Outside of water, that was all the birds received. It was better than nothing but far from a completely nutritious diet.

From that holding facility I visited another a week or so later that was owned by a different importer. This one had forty good-looking hyacinths. Their diet was completely different, consisting of a soupy mash of rice, dog chow and hot water. Apparently the hyacinths devoured this avidly, though whether it was because they loved the soupy mess or they were hungry as heck, I am not sure. There were no other supplements offered.

We decided to travel to still another large holding facility run by a popular importer. This facility had about ten hyacinths in fairly good feather. All they received daily for sustenance was sunflower seeds and water.

None of the three facilities had a complete and thorough diet, though it must be noted that feather condition and general condition of the birds were affected little by the diet since all birds had just arrived. In due time all these diets would have had some visible effect on the hyacinths, but whether good or bad only time would tell. We cannot rave over such diets, nor can we put them all down. I would love to feed fresh coconut and Brazil nuts as supplements or treats, for example.

Heppie Callahan has seven parrots, one of which is her pet hyacinth macaw. She calls him the "Cactus Eater" because he ate her entire cactus collection on his arrival. If she adds a cactus to her greenhouse area, it disappears when she turns her back. How this hyacinth succeeds eating the cactus without getting needles stuck in his thick tongue is beyond me.

Hyacinth macaws, like other large macaws, are extremely capable of being trained for bird shows. They are good actors and are easily trained to ride bicycles, to roller skate and to perform various tricks. One of the leading bird trainers in the country is Rod Cathcart of Kansas City. His trained birds are handled with expertise from coast to coast and in Canada.

The large macaws are usually good breeders, and the hyacinth macaw likewise has proved to be a good breeder. I know of several aviculturists who have been very successful in breeding the hyacinth.

One such fortunate breeder in Ohio has a pair of ten-year-olds that are proven breeders. His pair uses a giant garbage can as their nest box. Shavings are used as a base in the bottom although the birds kick most of it out. They spend three to four weeks preparing to go to nest by displaying to each other, the female squatting on a perch, shivering her wings. Copulation takes place frequently, with the male mounting the female. Finally, the male and female both enter the nest box and remain there for long periods of time. The male comes out periodically to eat and returns to feed the female. Two eggs are laid.

After approximately thirty days, the chicks hatch. Since the owner wishes to hand-raise the young to be "super tame," they are removed for hand-feeding. He utilizes sunflower hearts, canned oatmeal baby food, ground carrot and Meritene (a canned powdered vitamin and mineral supplement) to which is added hot water and the whole thing blended and heated before serving. Apparently the babies grow fast and well with this formula. Fledging seems to take place soon when babies are properly hand-fed. It would be nice to have sufficient statistics to see if hand-fed babies always fledge quicker than parent-fed babies. I am prone to think parent-fed babies would do better, but some macaw breeders say that hand-fed baby macaws grow and fledge faster.

Jim Sakawaya from New Mexico tells me he has a pair of hyacinth macaws that produce three eggs about once per year and hatches all three. This is exciting to hear, since my experiences with macaws have always involved two eggs per clutch. Other aviculturists have usually mentioned two eggs also. It would be interesting to secure additional statistics from other hyacinth breeders about clutch size.

A beautiful trio of hyacinth macaws.

Size and brilliance of color make hyacinths a featured attraction at bird parks.

The rich cobalt-blue of the outer plumage of a hyacinth macaw changes to dark gray, almost black, on the undersides of its wings.

The potential of hyacinth macaws as pets was first recognized by Brazilian natives.

Red-fronted Macaw, *Ara rubrogenys*

In 1973, the red-fronted macaw was thought to be extinct by some of the foremost ornithologists and aviculturists in the world. It was an almost unknown bird in the early decades of this century. Ornithologists believed it to be a rare bird of unknown habits from some part of Bolivia. Then, in 1974, a troop of adventurers going through the jungles of Bolivia happened to come upon a beautiful river basin. In this river basin was seen a rare hummingbird never before described, in addition to at least two rare and beautiful undescribed orchids.

It was in this basin that the red-fronted macaw was seen in groups of two to about a dozen, flying freely through the trees as well as feeding among the acacias and other trees. At first the participants were unable to identify the macaw as to species since so little had ever been recorded on *Ara rubrogenys*. Two years later, however, the first group of imported red-fronted macaws came into the United States. The price was drastically high, ranging from about $3,000.00 to $5,000.00 each.

I well remember the first pair I saw, in a very nice large aviary in Virginia. At first glance I almost thought I was looking at a thick-billed parrot, since the room was quite dark, but I soon realized that for the first time in my life I was looking at a pair of extremely rare red-fronted macaws. The owner, who happened to be one of the foremost American bird brokers, told us that this pair was slated to go to a major zoological society to serve as a breeding nucleus. Eventually, I am told, the pair did end up in the zoological collection, but whether they have produced young is not known to me.

For two or three years the red-fronted macaw remained for sale in very small quantities at $2,000.00 to $4,000.00 each, then, as suddenly as their rediscovery, the price came down to $700.00 to $800.00 each. This was in 1979-1980.

In my studies of the red-fronted macaw at Peabody Museum of Yale University and at the Los Angeles County Museum of Natural History, I found the red-fronted macaw to be a most unusual and beautiful parrot. The head and neck of this macaw are light green in color fading to a darker green body color. The forehead, crown, cheeks and an extensive area in the bend of the wing are rich orange-red. Wing coverts and thighs are orange, the tail is a dark green ending in dark

The red-fronted exhibits a rich orange color at the bend of the wing and on the front and crown.

Ara militaris mexicana, one of the three subspecies of the military macaw. Some experts consider *mexicana* a doubtful subspecies because the only difference between *mexicana* and the nominate subspecies is size.

This green-winged macaw enjoys close contact with its owner. Most macaws have gentle dispositions, and it doesn't take long before they allow such handling.

These three macaws, two scarlet and a blue and gold (each with at least one wing clipped), are well trained and can be trusted to remain on their perch even when it is placed outdoors.

blue, and the primary feathers are blue. These varied colors produce a magnificent bird. The facial patch is smaller than the patch on the other large macaws, and there are lines of tiny brown feathers through the patch. The bill and legs are dark gray.

The red-fronted macaw is the smallest of the ten large macaw species. The hyacinth is the largest, with the green-winged, scarlet and blue and gold next in size. The military is somewhat smaller but still two or three inches larger than the red-fronted. Yet all are considered part of the group of large macaws.

On a visit to a holding facility of one of the very large bird importers, I was amazed to see around thirty very nice-looking red-fronted macaws. These were maintained in large colony-type aviaries. I inquired about the food preferences of the red-fronted macaw, as compared with the other large macaws. I was told that the only difference noted was a greedy devouring of citrus fruits, particularly oranges, lemons and grapefruits. Otherwise, they enjoyed sunflower and safflower seeds, dry dog food and other vegetables. They seem to be a very tame macaw, not very flighty but calm.

A very good friend from Connecticut has one pair of most colorful red-fronted macaws. These appear to be young birds, perhaps much too young for breeding success. However, the owner has placed a nesting log in the aviary just in case the pair of red-fronteds become interested. They have shown no interest in breeding to date. His feeding program is somewhat different from others. He does feed safflower seeds and fresh fruit, but the main course is a mixture of chopped chicory, corn meal, millet seeds, hulled sunflower seeds, eggs and milk—all baked in the oven. This recipe is somewhat similar to a recipe I utilize for many of my parrots.

To the best of my knowledge, no red-fronted macaws have been bred in the United States. However, it must be stressed that anything can happen in the world of birds without publication. This truth hit me directly not too long ago. The American Federation of Aviculture has a breeders' directory which should do much good in developing a listing of rare parrots and perhaps matching individuals for potential matings. A friend of mine in New Hampshire refuses to become involved in any breeders' directory and wishes to be anonymous in his breeding successes. It is apparent that there are other good, dedicated aviculturists who have similar desires. This friend has a breeding accomplishment that few people today can boast of: his pair of Leadbeater's cockatoos produced three very beautiful babies in the fall of 1980. I suggested that such an occurrence most certainly deserves some recognition, but he made it very clear that he wanted nothing to do with any recognition.

The point I wish to make is that there are numerous aviculturists in this category. One cannot blame dedicated aviculturists for being shy and protective. Consequently, there may well be more red-fronted macaws around, and there may be some that have already produced young.

The red-fronted macaw is now considered threatened again, and its only chance at survival is probably a captive-bred nucleus in the hands of aviculturists.

A military macaw and a hybrid.

Linnaeus may have named this macaw "militaris" in reference to its disposition, but the term is also apt for the plumage.

Caninde Macaw, *Ara caninde*

Perhaps half the general public can differentiate the blue and gold macaw from other macaws and give it its correct name, but only about 1% of that 50% will perhaps be able to differentiate the caninde macaw from the blue and gold. I have seen caninde macaws sold as blue and golds, but the caninde is a unique and separate species of macaw. It is indeed very similar to the blue and gold in general color, but the facial patch has extensive tiny green feather lines; the green on the forehead is more extensive than in the blue and gold and extends over the crown; and the sides of the neck, the throat and the upper breast are bright blue (there is only a narrow black strip at the throat of the blue and gold). The caninde comes from northern Argentina, Paraguay, Bolivia and parts of Brazil.

For years these macaws were brought into the United States as blue and golds and sold as blue and golds. I well remember walking into a pet shop in the late sixties to see a "blue and gold" for sale. The bird just did not look right to me so I studied it for a very long period. Then I realized that tiny green facial feathers did not normally exist on the blue and gold. I had recalled that in the typical blue and gold these rows of tiny feathers were black. Upon further study, it was revealed that the bright blue throat and upper breast also did not exist in the blue and gold macaw, and it occurred to me that here was either a new type macaw or a new mutation. In time, with additional study, I realized that it was indeed a caninde macaw and not the closely related blue and gold.

We do not believe as others do that the caninde is a subspecies of the blue and gold. The caninde is definitely not a juvenile of the blue and gold—I have raised several baby blue and gold macaws and am very familiar with the juveniles, which look much like the adults. In 1973 there were occasional known caninde macaws for sale at $200.00 more than a blue and gold. In 1978 I noticed a pair for sale at $6,000.00. By 1979 and 1980 there were caninoides advertised for $10,000.00 and $20,000.00 per pair. Needless to say, few will be able to purchase them. A rarity such as this will have a variability of prices depending on demand and source of supply.

I know of a few individuals that own one or more caninde macaws. They make fine pets, are easily trained and have the ability to talk as well as any macaw. Billy Petts of Vermont owns a large caninde. This bird, called

Artistic representations of the head of a caninde macaw, *Ara caninde* (upper), and a blue and gold macaw, *Ara ararauna* (lower).

Though not as brilliantly colored as some of the other macaws, the military is still a fine looking bird and makes a wonderful pet.

Many people believe that the blue and gold macaw is more intelligent, and more mischievous, than all other macaws.

Claret, has an excellent vocabulary. His favorite saying is "Would you—a glass of sherry?". His owners are quite knowledgeable on wines, both imported and domestic, and I understand that Claret does not hesitate to take a nip—or sip.

There are few known captive breeding pairs of caninde macaws, although those in existence are in the hands of aviculturists who most certainly will successfully breed them in an effort to save them from becoming completely extinct. I have one friend in Florida who owns a very nice pair of caninde macaws. They are housed in a large planted aviary containing two large logs with nesting cavities. The macaws seem to enjoy the environment but have shown little interest in the nesting logs. They have a greater interest in the destruction of various plants and trees within their realm. Hopefully in due time they will reproduce.

Buffon's Macaw, *Ara ambigua*

A macaw that is often confused with the military macaw is the Buffon's. Buffon's macaw comes from Nicaragua, Costa Rica, Panama, Colombia and Ecuador, while the military macaw is not found in Central America countries but comes from Mexico and Colombia as well as scattered other parts of South America. Buffon's macaw is a larger macaw than the military by about six inches. One can easily differentiate the two by comparing the green color of the neck and back: the Buffon's color is much more yellowish green throughout. The red forehead is also paler, and the blue on the rump is a much lighter blue.

Information on the importation of Buffon's macaw is inadequate as many Buffon's are imported as military macaws. Many military macaws are sold as Buffon's intentionally, and a few Buffon's are sold as militaries by error. I will never forget the time I walked into a pet shop and saw a magnificent large light-colored Buffon's macaw. The price tag stated it was a tame military macaw, but upon studying it carefully, I was sure that it was a Buffon's. Considering the standards of the time, this bird was worth twice the price of a military. It is generally the pet shop owners who make errors in identification of the rarer psittacines.

There are a few aviculturists who have pairs of Buffon's macaws, and there are more pet owners with one or more. Harry Kapaun of Montana has a splendid specimen, this being his only bird. This macaw has the

Artistic representation of the head of *Ara ambigua,* Buffon's macaw.

The rewards of patience and good training are obvious. This scarlet macaw seems to find being on his back, a very unusual position for a bird, nothing out of the ordinary. A blue and gold and another scarlet seem to be patiently waiting their turn at such fun.

run of the ranch, inside and out. His wings are not clipped, so he is able to fly all over several acres. One can be sure that Harry (named after his owner) is always present at mealtime. His particularly fancy is bacon, generally at breakfast time. He also devours the warm home-baked bread that is fresh at every meal. Whenever human Harry rides his quarterhorse, he has the company of the Buffon's. Apparently this macaw enjoys the ride as well as anyone.

Two hyacinth macaws and a blue and gold macaw. The greater size of a hyacinth is emphasized by the fact that its head and neck appear much more massive than the head and neck of the blue and gold.

Penny Brooks of Pennsylvania has several macaws; as a matter of fact, she has just about every species of macaw available with the exception of two of the most rare. Her Buffon's is well-trained, having been part of a bird show at one of the large resorts. His favorite pastime involves answering the phone, even if it doesn't ring. He picks up the receiver and properly says, "Hello, call again sometime." He and the other macaws love to perch in an old pine tree, each bird having his own selected branch. Other than an occasional squawk, they behave like lazy macaws. Perhaps you have seen a group of macaws at a zoo on a bare tree, typically lazy but contented, each on his own tree limb. Occasionally two perch together.

Hyacinths, the largest of the macaws, are among the easiest to tame and train. They make excellent pets.

A closely associated veterinarian friend of mine has a pair of breeding Buffon's macaws. He first purchased these macaws in 1966 as military macaws and for a dozen years considered them to be military macaws. He found out in 1970 that they were a true pair since they went into his fireplace and proceeded to kick around a few papers sitting there. They were normally free to roam about the whole house and had chewed two sofas, a chair, two windowsills and numerous other things. My vet friend was totally surprised when he noticed two eggs in the corner of the fireplace. Both birds became very mean, attempting to scare all persons away from the general area. They were left alone to incubate their eggs for what seemed to the owner to be an eternity. Surprisingly both eggs did hatch. One chick died within three days, but the other chick was readily fed by the parents to adulthood.

After the birds had had three successful nestings in the same fireplace, I visited my friend's home and was awed to notice that this was a pair of Buffon's. The owner was not only surprised but somewhat depressed, as he had sold all the young for a very reasonable fee as military macaws.

I must agree with this veterinarian that once a good thing has been started, do not manipulate it or you may stop all activity. This is why he allows the pair of birds to utilize the fireplace as the nesting area year after year. There hasn't been a fire in that fireplace for several years, not since long before the first nest.

His birds receive a cup of sunflower seeds each day and a large can of corn including its juices. Finely ground carrots mixed with cooked oatmeal plus added vitamins are devoured, and dog biscuits shaped like bones are available at all times.

Incidentally, canned corn and fresh corn on the cob are good for parrots and there are many aviculturists and pet owners who feed corn. Hard corn, however, is generally refused by macaws. Buffon's is no different—it too refuses hard corn but devours the soft.

Lear's Macaw, *Anodorhynchus leari*

Lear's macaw has been confused with the hyacinth macaw through the centuries. One has to be very particular in viewing each bird to properly differentiate the two. Of course, the hyacinth is extremely large at about 40 inches long, while Lear's macaw is only 34 to 35 inches in length. Lear's macaw has a head and neck that are distinctly grayish blue although the general body is a beautiful dark hyacinth blue. In the hyacinth macaw the body, head and neck are all dark hyacinth blue. The glaucous macaw is similar to Lear's in size but has the head and neck the same dull blue shade as the body.

Lear's macaw is most definitely a very rare parrot. I know of eleven in the United States. Four of them are in two pairs, and there is possibly another pair at the San Diego Zoo, but it has been some time since I saw the San Diego collection. For many years, whenever a shipment of hyacinths arrived at importers, zoos, etc., there were many times included one or two Lear's macaws. In 1977 and 1978 there were occasional price listings that included Lear's macaws at $10,000 to $20,000 each.

I know of one elderly man who claims to have owned a pair of Lear's macaws since the late 1930's. They had produced two babies on one occasion in the decade of the fifties, and another two babies were produced in the decade of the sixties. That was the extent of the breeding for that pair to date. The whereabouts of those four Lear's macaws today is unknown.

Hopefully the American Federation of Aviculture's breeders' directory will bring together pairs of the Lear's macaw so they can be bred and prevented from becoming extinct.

Lear's macaw is an extremely rare macaw, and unless these macaws are successfully bred in captivity, there is a danger that these macaws will meet the same fate as the Cuban macaw.

Glaucous Macaw, *Anodorhynchus glaucus*

Until recently thought to be extinct by many ornithologists and aviculturists, evidence now reveals that this bird could still be around in very small groups in Uruguay. However, to the best of my knowledge, the glaucous macaw is not in evidence at any aviary in the United States. Again, however, I say this with caution, because you never know who might have a rare pair within just miles of where you live.

It was brought to my attention that a pair (male and female) does exist in Europe, and I now correspond with this aviculturist owner quite frequently. His pair is domestic and tame beyond belief. They have been so successful in breeding that the owner is building up a flock that he will use as foundation stock.

Lear's macaw is often confused with the hyacinth macaw, a bird which is much larger. This is a Lear's macaw.

The glaucous macaw is a large bird, about 35 inches in length from the tip of the beak to the tip of the tail. Its color is blue with a greenish hue to it. The bare facial patch is yellow. The beak is grayish black. I have never seen a living glaucous, although I have seen an occasional birdskin.

My European friend gave me his feeding formula, which is somewhat intriguing. He mixes a mash out of turkey starter, cottage cheese, a variety of small seeds such as Italian millet and very hot water. When he feeds this mixture it is nice and warm.

He has no price on his glaucous macaw babies as they are not for sale. However, if there were a price, it would be in the five-figure range. This man also successfully breeds other rare and unusual psittacines including the golden conure.

Another interesting note concerning the glaucous macaw in Europe involves the growth and fledging of the young. My experience with large macaws shows that fledging generally occurs around 80 to 90 days, though we have had scarlet macaws that didn't appear from the nest hole for 92 days. My European correspondent has indicated that his glaucous macaws constantly fledge at 120 days, which is about the longest period I have heard of.

Could it be that this small nucleus of glaucous macaws is the only one left in the world, wild or otherwise? This must give us all something to think about.

Artistic representation of the head of the glaucous macaw, *Anodorhynchus glaucus.*

Opposite:
Overgrown claws should be trimmed with dog claw clippers, or they can be shaped with a grindstone (above). A file may also be used to smooth any rough edges that remain after clippers are used (below).

Many macaw owners clip at least one wing of their bird in order to prevent the bird from flying away and to make the bird easier to handle and train.

Miniature Macaws

Yellow-collared Macaw, *Ara auricollis*

One of the most popular of the miniature macaws, the yellow-collared or yellow-naped macaw is readily available through most importers and brokers in the United States. I recall that in 1975 and 1976 yellow-collared macaws were selling for $400.00 to $500.00 each. By 1980 one could purchase a yellow-collared for $125.00 to $130.00 wholesale and double or triple that retail.

There are two types of yellow-collared macaws. The common type is basically a dark green bird. The front crown and cheek patches are brownish black, and the hindcrown and part of the nape have a bluish tinge to the feathers. The yellow collar is variable in individual birds; it generally encircles the entire back of the neck but is more extensive in some birds. The primary wing feathers are blue; the tail feathers are brownish red extending to blue. The facial patch is bare and white in color. The bill is grayish black.

The other type has a more brownish green tone to the ground color of the body. The collar, however, is a brilliant orange. This is a most fascinating and beautiful type, but one sees such birds only occasionally. It could possibly represent a distinct subspecies.

It happened that both color types were present at the 1980 National Bird Show at Jacksonville, Florida. The quality of the second type was high—the brilliant orange collar was striking. It was also noteworthy to mention that the "orange-collared macaw" was judged best of all the yellow-collared macaws and went on to be one of the finalists of the parrot show.

One frequently sees specimens of the yellow-collared macaw at the various bird exhibitions. The miniature macaws are easily shown and are unique little show birds that are often in good condition. At one show in which I officiated as judge, there were thirteen yellow-collared macaws entered, but not one was of the orange-collared variety.

As a pet, the yellow-collared macaw is quite adaptable and pleasant to have around. They are fairly easily tamed, and it is also likely that they will speak.

Ina Collardi of New York has two yellow-collared macaws that each have a vocabulary of at least fifty words. They love to perch on their owner's

Opposite:
On some yellow-collared macaws, the color on the bird's nape is orange rather than yellow.

A pair of yellow-collared macaws.

Severe macaws are often available in the pet trade.

The red-bellied macaw is the largest of the small macaws—and possibly the ugliest of all the macaws.

shoulders—one always prefers the left shoulder, the other prefers the right. They enjoy riding a miniature seesaw for hours at a time and attempt to drink out of the aquarium, something I would not recommend.

Another friend in Milwaukee has a single yellow-collared that insists on walking on the piano keys, apparently loving the sound it makes. When music is played the bird always sways back and forth as if dancing to the tune. This yellow-collared's name is Peter. He loves candied popcorn so much his owner has him trained to dance for it.

A nice young couple in Maine also own yellow-collareds; in fact, they have a pair. They live in the country where there are numerous trees around their property, including some very large pines. It is their habit to release the yellow-collared macaws each morning so they can have complete freedom the entire day. This, of course, only occurs during the summer months. They ensure the birds' return by feeding in the early evening within the open aviaries. Since sunflower seed is the macaws' favorite delicacy, this is what they receive in the evening. However, it is to no avail to attempt to coax them down from the high pines during the day, even with a delicacy. They seem to understand that their freedom is secure for an entire day. It is interesting to note, however, their rapid retreat to their aviary whenever a severe thunderstorm develops. They particularly seemed to enjoy the pine nuts that they occasionally locate. That they never flew beyond sight of the aviary does not surprise me, because I have always been of the opinion (from experience) that parrots could not find their way back home once they flew beyond about a quarter of a mile away from their origin.

I had a golden cherry lovebird that flew away and two days later returned to eat outside the aviary. We caught that one and still have him today. Another bird I lost flew away for a couple days to return because of hunger. This was a chattering lory. Our neighbors reported that they saw a large red bird being chased about by four or five cardinals. This chattering lory was happy to get back home! However, I have heard of no other returns except for these two yellow-collared macaws.

The yellow-collared macaw has now been successfully bred in captivity, and I know of several successful pairs throughout the United States. One such pair, owned by a very large private aviary, is utilizing an apple tree log for a nesting place. The pair had a choice between the hollow apple log and a larger hollow oak log. They didn't even look at the oak, though much time was spent inspecting the apple tree.

Apparently the miniature macaws go to nest at an earlier age than the large macaws, but we do not have sufficient data to really know all of the facts. The pair mentioned above was very young when purchased, perhaps under one year. However this is most difficult to tell. At any rate, they went to nest just three years after they were purchased, which would make them at least four years old or perhaps a little older. One can never be sure of the age of newly purchased birds unless a complete history accompanies them.

They laid two eggs on the first try but neither egg hatched. In another six months they attempted another nest. This time three eggs were laid, but again none of the eggs hatched. In another year they laid two eggs, and this time both chicks hatched. The chicks were removed from the nest for hand-feeding and now are doing very well as young adults.

Severe Macaw, *Ara severa*

Severe macaws, also called chestnut-fronted macaws, are perhaps the most widely kept of the miniatures, although not the ones most in demand (there is perhaps a greater demand for Illiger's macaw). The severe macaw is quite colorful. The front is a chestnut brown blending into the bluish green crown. The nape and general body color are green. The wing primaries and primary wing coverts are blue, there is much red at the bend of the wing and the underwing coverts are red. The undersides of the tail are brownish red, while the vent underfeathers are light blue. The bare facial patch has several rows of tiny black feathers. The beak is dark gray, as are the legs.

There are two subspecies of this macaw. The nominate race, *Ara severa severa,* is 21 to 22 inches long, while the other subspecies, *Ara severa castaneifrons,* is 25 to 26 inches in length. There are no color differences. *Ara severa severa* is found in Venezuela, Guyana, Surinam and Brazil. *Ara severa castaneifrons* comes from Panama and Colombia.

Many severe macaws have been imported into the United States in the last few years. In 1975, severe macaws were selling for $400.00 to $500.00 each wholesale. By 1979 they were down to $135.00 to $150.00 wholesale.

Because of the brown shading the front of the birds, severe macaws are also known as chestnut-fronted macaws.

Opposite:
Severe macaws are pleasant, colorful birds which, when properly trained, make excellent pets.

One of the saddest and one of the happiest bird events I remember involved a severe macaw, Spanky, a most cherished bird who loved to talk. He particularly loved to say "pretty bird" and then climb to one's shoulder. He loved to kiss humans. Yet one lovely summer day when his outside summer aviary was opened for feeding he flew over my shoulder to the top of a large oak tree. Within hours he disappeared, never to be seen again.

Spanky had an interesting history, having been selected out of a nest in Guyana and sold in a farmers' market in Georgetown. In Georgetown he was purchased as a brand new youngster by a visiting American from Cincinnati for just a mere $5.00. This was in the mid-sixties. The man from Cincinnati returned to the U.S. and kept Spanky for a year until he had to return to South America. He then sold Spanky to Loretta White, who owned several pet shops. Spanky remained in one of the shops for two years until I saw him one day. Through a trade we came home with him and retained him for four years. Through these four years he became the pet of pets. When we took a two-year tour of the Caribbean we left Spanky with a very close friend, Dr. Bill Wiseman of Ohio. Bill also did wonders with Spanky and vice versa. On our return to the states, we again retrieved Spanky and kept him for another six years until the fateful day he decided to take flight.

Thus, as a pet, the severe macaw is not only attractive but quite intelligent and friendly. Earl Grossman of Massachusetts had a very friendly macaw that loved to come onto Earl's shoulder and arm. Macaws enjoy walking along one's arm to the shoulder. It tends to be a trait of macaws and parrots in general to climb to the highest point possible; occasionally they will climb to the top of one's head.

Another very outstanding pet is owned by Johnnie Bridk of Virginia. Johnnie prides himself on the fact that his macaw will fetch his slippers and his glasses on command. The bird will then sit on the chair just above Johnnie's head for long periods of time. Johnnie swears the bird can read the newspaper with him! This severe macaw, named Pedroni, simply loves oranges. Johnnie believes this bird will eat oranges in preference to sunflower seeds.

We have another acquaintance who lost his severe macaw to an untimely death. The autopsy associated the death with the overfeeding of sunflower seeds of the oily kind, perhaps the small black variety. Indeed, there are different varieties of sunflower seeds. The best type is the large gray seed, although the gray and black seed is worthwhile. However, the small solid black seed is thought to have too much oil. Whether or not death or even sickness can be attributed to oily sunflower seeds will be determined only after more evidence has been secured.

We have also heard rumors to the effect that citrus fruits are dangerous to psittacines. Personally, I believe this one to be an old wives' tale. I have fed much citrus in the form of oranges, lemons, limes and grapefruits with no trouble in the last 25 years. Figs, if available, as well as dates are entirely nutritious for your severe macaws and all other parrots.

The severe macaw has been bred in captivity. Certainly there are several breeding pairs throughout this country, a few of which are familiar to me.

My own breeding pair has selected an oak log with a large hollow area. I placed black greenhouse dirt for two to three inches in the bottom and then three inches of shavings. They kick out most of the shavings when getting ready to nest and then proceed to fool around for three or four weeks before finally laying an egg. I have never seen more than two eggs from this pair; however, other breeders have indicated that up to three eggs may be laid by their severe macaws at times. In each case my severes have successfully hatched both babies, fed them to maturity and fledged them in 70 to 80 days. Incubation of the eggs varied from 28 to 30 days (if I counted correctly).

In season they love sunflower seeds, cucumbers, corn on the cob, cheese, canned dog food and pound cake as well as whole-wheat bread soaked in milk. They also feed well on the usual cut-up fruit pieces. We also include slices of fresh oranges and grapefruits.

Red-bellied Macaw, *Ara manilata*

Perhaps the ugliest as well as the largest of the miniature macaws is the red-bellied macaw. In my opinion, its yellow facial patch adds to its ugliness. The general plumage is green on the neck and back with a slight olive brown tone. The cheeks are bluish green, but the throat and breast feathers are grayish green edged with blue. There is a large red area on the abdomen and near the vent. The undertail coverts are blue-green. The primaries and primary wing coverts are blue and the secondary coverts are brownish green. The tail is green above, yellowish green below. The beak and legs are grayish black.

While visiting Surinam on the coastal area, I was fortunate to see several flocks of red-bellied macaws flying over the palm groves. Occasionally a group would land in the palms. They were extremely difficult to detect,

Though it may be "short on" looks, the red-bellied is "long on" personality and makes a good pet.

The naked yellow facial patch and the overall dull coloring of the red-bellied macaw are in sharp contrast to the brilliant coloring of such other macaws as the scarlet.

Larry Brandt is proud of his new young red-bellied macaw.

although one would have thought that the red belly would be more visible.

When in Guyana, I searched for the red-bellied again to no avail. I was told that I might find them in the botanical gardens, so we took a tour with no success. We did see several birds, including a few psittacines, but no red-bellied macaws. We were there around noon and were later told that most are seen there in the late afternoon.

The red-bellied macaw is common in nature, but it is less frequently seen than nobles, severes, or yellow-collareds. Whether they are not as popular or are more difficult to secure, one seldom finds them on import listings. Brokers who generally claim they can get anything you desire (that isn't endangered) do not seem to be able to secure the red-bellied macaw. One importer told me that the red-bellied macaw was difficult to obtain since they were not frequently collected in the countries from which he made his imports. He also indicated that the price was prohibitive for that type of bird. Other psittacines, he implied, were more in demand.

Undoubtedly there are many red-bellied macaws at various aviaries, but I know of only eight pairs and don't know of a single red-bellied kept as a pet. Of the eight pairs of red-bellied macaws, not one of them has even attempted to go to nest. Six of the eight pairs have nesting boxes or logs in their aviaries, yet to no avail. In each case, however, with two exceptions, all birds are comparatively young. One pair is six years of age but is being fed a straight sunflower seed diet which might account for lack of breeding. The single pair that shows evidence of some interest is about ten years of age. Although they don't go to nest, they at least look into the nesting facility.

Bob Andrews of Rhode Island had a nice pair of red-bellied macaws that entered their nest box showing all signs of breeding. About the time Bob was having thoughts of good luck, he found the female dead at the base of the nest. It was that close! Upon post-mortem examination, a large egg was found in the oviduct. She had died of egg binding.

Noble Macaw, *Ara nobilis*

There are two subspecies of the noble macaw, also called the red-shouldered macaw. One subspecies, *Ara nobilis nobilis,* varies from 10 to 12 inches in length. The other subspecies, *Ara nobilis cumanensis,* is larger by almost three inches but does not vary from the nominate race in morphology or color. The bare facial patch is white. The front and forecrown are blue blending into green. The general plumage is green, more yellowish under the wings, tail and lower abdomen. The bend of wings and underwing coverts are red. The wing feathers are mostly green with some blue color. The legs and beak are grayish black.

While visiting Blue Ridge Aviaries in Virginia, I was quite impressed by the numerous specimens of the noble macaw that they had on their premises. I was particularly intrigued by one group that was not over ten inches long and perhaps even less. They were the cutest, tiniest macaws I recalled seeing in a long time. It was apparent that this aviary had both subspecies. One doesn't see too many of the nominate race—apparently the larger subspecies is more often available.

I know of several pet noble macaws in various homes. They make an ideal pet; though quite noisy, they are friendly when tamed.

Billy and Queen are owned by Ed Wait of New York. They are just pets, according to Ed. They love to fly throughout the home, particularly in the greenhouse just off their kitchen. They enjoy landing on and partially destroying the giant hibiscus plant. They spend an equal amount of time on a large gardenia plant, but surprisingly it still blooms. Their feeding dishes are in the greenhouse, which is rather frustrating to the person cleaning the greenhouse. Of course an occasional sunflower starts growing in the greenhouse, and Ed has a good idea how it started.

A small group of noble macaws sitting close together and preening each other.

Opposite:
The noble macaw is the smallest of all the macaws. It is a cute, perky bird which can be tamed to make a fine pet.

Both subspecies of the noble macaw have bred in captivity. The noble macaw is unusual among macaws because it has been known to lay as many as five eggs per nesting, though I personally do not know of any that hatched all five.

One breeder in Connecticut, who wishes to remain anonymous, has two pairs of *Ara nobilis nobilis.* Both pairs have been owned for ten years. There are three nesting boxes in each aviary, giving each pair sufficient choice. In the case of the first pair, they selected a pine box in the shape of a grandfather clock. The owner had it arranged so he could open the box in the rear as a peep hole. On his first look, there were no eggs, only a few scraps of shavings as a result of chewing. A week later the box was again checked; this time there were two solid white eggs. A week later he was surprised to see five eggs in the nest. Both parents remained inside the nest most of the time. The male apparently would leave the nest for feeding, then return to feed the female by regurgitation. Whenever the owner put cheese of any type out, however, the female would leave the nest to eat. This was possibly her favorite food.

The other pair selected a small garbage can half-full of cedar shavings. They kicked out all of the shavings and proceeded to spend much time in the nest. By the end of a two-week period they had produced three eggs. This pair spent a lot of time feeding outside of the nest, but both birds entered the nest frequently. Both birds slept in the can all night, probably sharing the incubation. Feeding practices, in addition to cheese, included apples, grapes, canned corn, freshly baked bread, sunflower seeds, safflower seeds and millet seeds.

The first pair hatched only two chicks, two eggs were infertile and the fifth egg had a chick dead in the shell. Both chicks were raised to maturity by the parents. The second pair hatched two out of three, the third egg being infertile. Only one of these chicks survived to maturity; the other died at about two weeks. Again these were raised by the parents.

In our writings we say much about the successes, but there are also many depressing incidents where nest after nest of young birds is lost. On numerous occasions there are eggs that never hatch. Some of these indicate fertility problems, while others are humidity problems where the chick cannot penetrate the shell because it is so very dry. Occasionally chicks will hatch but the parents may not feed properly or may not feed at all. Then the chicks will die. The saddest thing that can happen is when chicks die at three to four weeks of age. One man mentioned to me that that was when he wished he had removed the chicks for hand-feeding.

Unfortunately, noble macaws have a tendency to be a bit noisier than other macaws.

Harry Harris of New York has a pair that is at least seven years of age. They nest in an old wine barrel at least twice a year with success at hatching two babies each time. The parents are rested sufficiently though, since the babies are removed for hand-feeding. We asked Harry for his formula for feeding the babies, and he suggested that his formula was somewhat off the beaten path. He starts with powdered Esbilac, a bitch supplement, to which he adds hot water, ground apples, ground sunflower hearts, cottage cheese and whole wheat bread. This all goes into a blender. The soupy mixture is spoon-fed warm to the babies. He claims they do very well on this mixture. When they are about five weeks of age he adds various varieties of dog food (canned) to the mixture in the blender, thereby increasing their protein.

Illiger's Macaw, *Ara maracana*

About one inch shorter than the severe macaw, the Illiger's is perhaps the most colorful of all the miniature macaws. Often called the blue-winged macaw by those of meager knowledge, this name is really a poor one since so many macaws and other parrots have blue wings or blue primaries. The facial mask is pale yellow. The red forehead is characteristic, blending into a bluish crown with bluish green cheeks and throat. The general body color is olive green; the undertail color is yellowish green. There is a bright red abdomen and a red lower rump. This is a very colorful miniature macaw.

Illiger's is most popular in avicultural circles but less popular in pet circles. Although Illiger's is still fairly common in Brazil, Paraguay and parts of Argentina, it is seldom imported. During the years 1979 and 1980 there weren't over 200 Illiger's imported into the entire country. Most of those that were imported made their way very quickly to aviculturists' homes and breeding units. A nice exhibit of Illiger's macaws is seen at Busch Gardens in Tampa, Florida. They are in a pleasantly attractive display. I know of no private pet Illiger's, although one really never knows who may have something.

I am familiar with about four different pairs of Illiger's macaw in various corners of the country. One pair in North Dakota has been owned for about six years. The owners have no idea what sex their birds are.

Left: A pair of Illiger's macaws. Macaws are avid chewers of wood, as evidenced by the condition of the tree in this photo. *Below:* These military macaws will be able to do little damage to their perch or the aviary; both are metal. *Opposite:* This green-winged macaw is busy demolishing his perch. Such wooden perches in a macaw aviary have to be replaced periodically.

Hybrid macaws bathing. Among macaws, interspecific hybrids vary considerably in coloration; as a result, it is often impossible to identify the parent species from the appearance of the offspring.

However, they have also not attempted to coax their birds to breed—they have not placed nest boxes in their aviary, which is an entire room of their home. They also have two male severe macaws in this room, but the Illiger's stay to themselves and away from the severes. Since the owners raise sunflower seeds by the ton, they have few feeding problems. They also raise a limited amount of safflower seeds just for their birds.

Another pair with which I am familiar is owned by a very charming family in Florida. They are indeed fortunate, as their birds are in outside aviaries within an orange grove. Their birds have plenty of room. All the birds are on wire above the ground. Two nest boxes made of wood are in each aviary. The pair of Illigers has gone to nest, laying two eggs once; however, neither hatched. The owners are eagerly awaiting another return to the nest.

The third pair of Illiger's with which I am familiar are based in Rhode Island. They, too, use an entire spare room in a beautiful old mansion. Extremely attractive nest boxes grace the room. Not only are they attractive, but they seem to be useful. The pair of Illiger's is alone in the room. They have gone to nest on three occasions, raising a total of five young. In the second nest there were two eggs; one failed to hatch. Two chicks hatched and were raised from the final nesting.

Another pair of Illiger's is located in an apartment high over Boston. They are unsexed and have not been offered nesting boxes. Their owners plan to introduce them to a nesting can within the next year.

Currently, the Fish and Wildlife Service of the U.S. Department of Interior is asking that the Illiger's macaw be listed as threatened. They do this with meager knowledge. Unless certain psittacines are allowed to be bred by aviculturists, they will disappear from their normal habitats, not due to importations, but because of the encroachment of deforestation, planting of banana and coconut plantations, lumbering, and building of new cities and towns. A few writers fail to understand that aviculturists, who have proved themselves time after time, are the *only ones* who can save many species from extinction. History is going to prove that the Fish and Wildlife Service has blundered time after time in preventing aviculturists from receiving and breeding the rare and endangered species that are not going to thrive today in their natural habitats. Aviculturists have saved at least four, and probably more, birds: the turquoisine parakeet, the scarlet-chested parakeet (both bred readily in captivity), the Bali mynah and the Nene goose.

Blue-headed Macaw, *Ara couloni*

Another of the miniature macaws, the blue-headed, is perhaps the rarest of all the miniatures (except the Spix's), at least in the United States. Only rarely have I seen the blue-headed macaw advertised on importer or broker listings. I have never seen a blue-headed macaw in a zoo, nor have I seen the blue-headed macaw in a pet shop.

Coming from Peru and western Brazil, the blue-headed macaw is another very attractive bird. The entire head and neck are blue; the facial patch is bluish gray. The lower neck and general body color are olive green. Primaries and primary coverts are blue. The upper tail is rust, ending in blue. The color under the wings and tail is yellowish green. The beak and legs are gray; often the tip of the bill is light gray.

This 20-inch macaw is in the hands of only a few aviculturists. My searches have located three owners, only one with a true mated pair. To the best of my knowledge, the blue-headed macaw has not been bred in the United States.

The one pair of blue-headed macaws was located in the state of Maine. This aviculturist has only six birds, two pairs of amazons plus this pair of blue-headed macaws. The owner has them in a large cage with a wooden nest box attached. They show no interest in the nest box. Even the amazons' interest in the nest box in the next cage has no effect on the blue-headed macaws.

There is much to be learned about the blue-headed macaw. Hopefully enough of them will be allowed into this country so aviculturists can show what they can do as devoted breeders.

Spix's Macaw, *Cyanopsitta spixii*

A small macaw, one of the miniatures, the Spix's or little blue macaw is about 25 inches long measured from the tip of the beak to the tip of the tail. The Spix's is extremely rare and found only in Brazil. Since they are classified as endangered, and since Brazil has now prevented their exportation, there can be no wild-caught imports even if they could be found in the wild. There are, however, a few breeding pairs throughout the world.

This is a most attractive little macaw. The forehead, cheeks, crown and ear coverts are gray with a blue tinge.

Spix's macaws are very rare, very attractive miniature macaws. These are two young Spix's.

Artistic representations of the head of a Spix's macaw, *Cyanopsitta spixii* (left), and a blue-headed macaw, *Ara couloni* (right).

Several different types of nest boxes have been used to successfully breed macaws. This pair of scarlet macaws is using a barrel placed high in their aviary.

The upper throat is bluish gray, while the breast and rump are dark blue. The wings and tail are very dark blue. The underside of the tail is dark gray. The most unusual (and beautiful) characteristic involves the eye ring and the lores, which are bare and black. Beak and legs are grayish black.

There are three known pairs of Spix's macaws in the United States, all owned by aviculturists and all breeding. I have never seen a Spix's at a zoo, although I have not visited every zoo in the United States. There are also several pairs of Spix's in Europe. One dealer in England offered me a pair of Spix's macaws for twenty thousand dollars in 1979.

The Spix's macaw is perhaps one of the most awesome yet beautiful of the macaws. In particular, a breeding pair is most attractive. One pair in Belgium has been most prolific: they have successfully produced three young each year for the past six years. Apparently, a good share of the progeny go to England for sale. The Spix parents have a mean look about them, partly because of the black facial area about the eyes. However, as parents they are not as pugnacious as some of the larger macaws.

Our Belgian friend utilizes a wooden "grandfather clock" nest box for his pair of Spix's. Surprising to me, his macaws do not seem to chew the wooden nest box. There is no easy way to peek into the box to count the eggs, to see just how the young are doing or to see if there are any dead ones. This could be good since too often aviculturists love to "peek" in at the nesting parents. It is also a good practice not to allow strangers into your breeding aviaries. Firstly, birds immediately recognize when strangers are present. This frightens many birds, sometimes causing them to leave their nests. Secondly, strangers may have just come from another aviary or their own and might possibly be mechanical carriers of disease.

The Spix's macaw has also been successfully bred in Germany. It is interesting to note that European and South African aviculturists are years ahead of the United States in success in breeding many species of parrots.

The few Spix's in the United States are well-kept secrets, and rightfully so because we have entered an era of thievery of birds. Aviculturists have to be very cautious to prevent birds in their collections from being stolen.

Hybrids and Extinct Macaws

Of all the species of parrots, there are none in the world that have produced as many hybrids as the macaws. This, of course, is not true in the wild but in captivity. My personal opinion is against hybridizing of macaws and parrots in general; however, it is being done extensively with macaws. There are two main reasons why hybrids occur. Firstly, when several macaws are maintained together, they tend to pair off, many times pairing off with a macaw of a different species. Man should be in greater control of this, preventing the mixing of species. The other reason involves single birds and a lack of aviary space. Such a single bird of one species may be put with a single bird of another species, and before you know it, they are breeding. If indeed we are going to breed species to prevent extinction, we must also attempt not to hybridize.

One hybrid has been bred so readily that it has been named for several years. This is the "Catalina macaw." This hybrid is a cross between *Ara macao,* the scarlet macaw, and *Ara ararauna,* the blue and gold macaw. One has to admit that the brilliant orange breast, the black tiny feathers across the facial patch, and the blue head, neck and back are colorful. The wings are generally blue to bluish green. We see many "Catalina macaws" and other hybrids at various bird shows, at bird gardens with performing birds and occasionally at zoos.

Other hybrids that I have seen involved crosses between the scarlet macaw and the military, the blue and gold and the green-winged, and the blue and gold with the military. All of these are from the same genus. Interestingly, I have also seen about four specimens that were hybridized between two different genera. These were from the hyacinth macaw crossed with the blue and gold macaw *(Anodorhynchus x Ara).* Every one of these hybrids had the nastiest disposition and temper I have ever seen in a macaw, yet it is noteworthy that both the hyacinth and the blue and gold have good temperaments!

When reading this chapter, just think of what additional species and subspecies might be added to this list one hundred years from now. What a sad shame that the following species can no longer be seen by aviculturists and bird lovers the world over. Some of the information we have on extinct macaws is very sketchy, and it is possible that many more existed that we have no records of at all.

This hybrid macaw is known as a "shamrock" macaw. It is a cross between a scarlet and a military macaw.

A "Catalina" macaw—the result of a cross between a scarlet macaw and a blue and gold macaw.

This beautifully colored hybrid is a cross between a green-winged macaw and a scarlet macaw.

The most recent macaw to become extinct (in the late 1800's) was *Ara tricolor,* the Cuban macaw. This was a fabulously beautiful macaw about 23 inches long, with a clear white facial patch. The entire head, neck, throat, upper breast, thighs and abdomen were all bright orange. The bend of the wings and upper wing coverts were brown, with each feather edged in orange. The primary and secondary wing feathers were dark blue. The tail was rusty red ending in blue. The bill was dark gray.

Apparently the last *Ara tricolor* was killed near the southern coast of Cuba in 1864, according to a 1905 summary by Bangs and Zappey. It was thought however, that the macaw might still be found alive in a few swamps in Cuba as late as 1890.

It was written by Oviedo that Columbus reported several red macaws on various Caribbean islands. *Ara guadeloupensis* was described by various French authors as well as Columbus. This macaw apparently was smaller than *Ara macao* but similar in coloring except for a bright red tail. The Carib indians called the large red parrots "guacamayas" according to Columbus; Columbus said they were "as big as chickens." These macaws were used for food by the Carib indians as well as kept as pets by the early European settlers. These factors undoubtedly led to their demise.

Rothschild described a yellow and blue macaw on the island of Martinique, calling it *Ara martinica.* It resembled our blue and gold macaw except for a yellow tail. Apparently this macaw was extremely rare even when first discovered. They were killed for their beautiful feathers and for food, and they were occasionally exported to Europe. It is thought that Columbus returned to Spain with some of these yellow and blue macaws to be displayed in various processions.

Ara gossei, named after the naturalist Gosse in 1847, was found in Jamaica and considered to be extremely rare. The forehead, crown and nape were bright yellow, but the sides of the face and back were bright scarlet. The wings were bright blue. This beautiful bird was soon eradicated one way or another.

Anodorhynchus purpurescens designates a large violet macaw found only in Guadeloupe. It was popular with the natives for its feathers as well as for food. Rothschild indicated that this bird was almost extinct by the time it was discovered by Europeans.

The above are birds that will never come back. We must ensure that the macaws of today reproduce in captivity so this will never happen again. We cannot wait for the so-called environmentalists to save them in the wild—because they will not be able to.

INDEX

Page numbers in parentheses refer to illustrations.

Anodorhynchus glaucus, See Glaucous macaw
Anodorhynchus hyacinthinus, See Hyacinth macaw
Anodorhynchus leari, See Lear's macaw
Anodorhynchus purpurescens, 124
Ara ambigua, See Buffon's macaw
Ara ararauna, See Blue and gold macaw
Ara auricollis, See Yellow-collared macaw
Ara caninde, See Caninde macaw
Ara chloroptera, See Green-winged macaw
Ara couloni, See Blue-headed macaw
Ara gossei, 124
Ara guadeloupensis, 124
Ara macao, See Scarlet macaw
Ara manilata, See Red-bellied macaw
Ara maracana, See Illiger's macaw
Ara martinica, 124
Ara militaris, See Military macaw
Ara nobilis, See Noble macaw
Ara rubrogenys, See Red-fronted macaw
Ara severa, See Severe macaw
Ara tricolor, See Cuban macaw
Aviaries, 19-20 (26, 36, 49)

Beak, trimming (40)
Blue and gold macaw, 11, 12, 54, 58-59 (7, 10, 13, 23, 24, 25, 27, 31, 38, 42, 43, 54, 55, 56, 57, 59, 60, 61, 66, 83, 86, 87, 89, 90)
Blue-headed macaw, 117
Breeding, 12, 22-23
Buffon's macaw, 11, 88, 90-91 (88)

Cages, 19
Caninde macaw, 11, 86, 88 (86)
Chestnut-fronted macaw, See Severe macaw
Classification, 11
Claws, trimming, 45 (44, 95)
Cuban macaw, 124
Cyanopsitta spixii, See Spix's macaw

Diet, 16, 18
Disease, symptoms of, 37

Egg binding, 41
Eggs, 12, 23
Exhibiting, 30-31
Extinct macaws, 121, 124

Feather plucking, 41, 45 (42)
Food receptacles (16)
Food supplements (18, 33, 37)

Geographic distribution, 11
Glaucous macaw, 11, 92, 94 (94)
Green-winged macaw, 11, 12, 62-63, 65 (12, 15, 29, 67, 70, 82, 115)

Hand-feeding, 27
Hyacinth macaw, 11, 73, 76-77 (7, 16, 74, 75, 77, 78, 79, 90, 91)
Hybrid macaws, 121, 122, 123 (20, 29, 35, 49, 84, 115)

Illiger's macaw, 113, 116 (114)

Lear's macaw, 11, 92 (92, 93)

Military macaw, 11, 12, 68-69, 72 (11, 69, 71, 81, 84, 85, 87, 114)

Nest boxes, 22-23 (22, 119)
Noble macaw, 109, 112-13 (110, 111, 112)

Parrot stand, 19 (17, 19)
Preening (43, 48)
Preventive medicine, 33, 37

Red-bellied macaw, 11, 105, 108-109 (34, 99, 106, 107, 108)
Red-fronted macaw, 11, 80, 83-84 (81)
Red-shouldered macaw, See Noble macaw

Scarlet macaw, 12, 47-51 (7, 14, 20, 21, 23, 24, 25, 28, 32, 36, 39, 46, 47, 48, 49, 50, 52, 53, 64, 66, 83, 89, 119)
Severe macaw, 11, 101, 104-105 (98, 102, 103)
Shipping crate (36)
Spix's macaw, 11, 117, 120 (118)

Training, 12, 49 (20)
T-stand, See Parrot stand

Vitamin deficiencies, 45
Vitamins, 33, 37

Wing clipping (95)

Yellow-collared macaw, 97, 100-101 (96, 98)

Handbook of Macaws
H-1044